Hershey

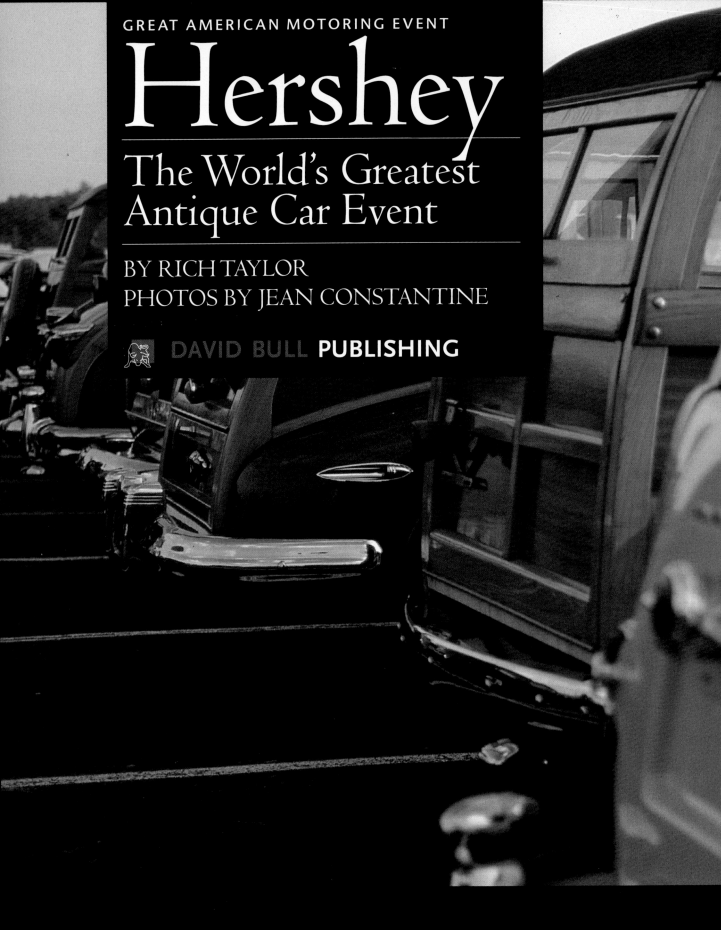

GREAT AMERICAN MOTORING EVENT

Hershey

The World's Greatest Antique Car Event

BY RICH TAYLOR

PHOTOS BY JEAN CONSTANTINE

DAVID BULL **PUBLISHING**

ISBN: 0-9649722-2-0

Printed in Korea.

Graphic concept and cover design by Tom Morgan, Blue Design.
Book Design by Jean Constantine, Taylor-Constantine, Inc.

10 9 8 7 6 5 4 3 2

David Bull Publishing
4250 E. Camelback Road
Suite K.150
Phoenix, AZ 85018
602-852-9500

Foreword

Hershey is mud, dust, rain and sun. But Hershey is also the Holy Days of the antique car hobby, the most important weekend of the year. People come from all over the world to our humble Pennsylvania fields to exchange ideas and thoughts, to buy and sell automobiles, to buy and sell automotive toys, to buy and sell automotive photographs and tools and parts.

Some of them come with the most exotic items you'd ever imagine, and some of them go home with exotic things. It's an exchange. Vendors search out special things that they will only take to Hershey because they know they'll find buyers who'll be interested in these special items, and buyers come knowing they'll find rare exotica they won't find anywhere else.

Of course, some people come just to "kick tires." They've been coming here for forty years, some of them, and they've gotten to the point where they're no longer interested in buying or selling. They come for Saturday's car show, to hear the race cars run. Or they just come to reminisce, to talk about the good old days, to meet friends they may not have seen since Hershey the year before. For them, especially, Hershey is Mecca.

ENTHUSIASTS BY THE hundreds of thousands flock to Hershey each year to enjoy the largest car show and swap meet in the world.

— *William H. Smith*
Executive Director
Antique Automobile Club of America

Introduction

Hershey has such visual impact. You drive down Airport Road, and as far as the eye can see there are old cars and parts. This sheer overwhelming size of Hershey is what always amazes first-time visitors. For example, each year I go to the big swap meet at the National Motor Museum in Beaulieu. This is the biggest swap meet in England—you could put it in a corner of Hershey and lose it! You can cover the entire Beaulieu swap meet in half a day. I spend four days at Hershey, and I still don't visit every field!

What interests me at Hershey is finding some nice, rare early stuff. It used to be, you could go to Hershey and you'd trip over pre-World War I brass lamps. Each year there are fewer and fewer. Today, because of the way our old car hobby has changed, Chevy accessories from 1957 are what people bring to Hershey.

The hobby is becoming very specialized. There are now specialty swap meets—there's one in Rhinebeck, New York in May, two weeks after the general swap meet—where you're not allowed to sell any post-1915 bits. It's like going to Hershey 40 years ago. For me, I was delirious. It was like being a young guy again, seeing all this stuff for the first time.

I think vendors who have a choice ought to be bringing their early Brass Era stuff to Hershey. They'd see a feeding frenzy, because there's just not enough of these beautiful pieces showing up at Hershey today. At Hershey, you get a lot of people from overseas who own early American automobiles, and they're coming to Hershey especially to look for this Brass Era stuff.

The fascination of Hershey is that if you look long enough and dig hard enough, you can find almost anything. It caters to literally everyone. Since they've liberalized the rules and allowed more postwar stuff, it's become a very useful event.

I think the single most interesting phenomenon I've observed at Hershey over the past ten or fifteen years is the rise of automobilia as a legitimate form of collecting. Automotive art, toys, buzz-bomb racers, things like that are tremendously popular now. They've become a really important part of the hobby. Why? Because there are an awful lot of people who live in condos today. The cars have gotten so expensive, as well. You can have a whole automobilia collection for the price of a single car.

Plus, there's the portability issue. The convenience. You can put a $50,000 Peter Helck painting under your arm and walk away. You don't need a trailer. I have quite a few automotive paintings, and as my former wife said, "The nice thing about these Helcks is they don't drip oil."

What attracts us to this stuff? Darned if I know. In my case, I was standing on a street corner when I was twelve, and a 1911 Buick drove by. I was imprinted by that Buick and just grew up liking old cars. That was at a time in the fifties when the hobby was just starting to grow, so I grew up along with it.

The attraction? All sorts of things—nostalgia, making a buck on the side, putting the car back together, collecting things for their own sake. Particularly at Hershey, you will see guys who come there just so they can be known as the guru who knows about Star and Durant automobiles, or whatever it is they know about. It's the opportunity for them to play the pundit, to have acolytes kneel at their feet to acquire their wisdom. To use a contemporary term, it makes them a *player*. "If you want to know about Star or Durant, I'm *the* expert. I'm *the* guy."

This cuts both ways. You can go to Hershey and find out why you have to have the accessory water pump, because your model of car always overheats without it. You can learn almost anything. You see guys with hats that say "Ask me about Graham-Paige" not "Ask me about my grandchildren." If you need to learn something about Graham-Paige, it's the place to learn.

For people in the east and midwest, Hershey is always a little sad because it signals the end of the hobby season. You know when you drive away on Sunday morning, that you'll have to go home and put your cars away for another winter. Hershey has its faults, but it's an enduring institution that I hope never ends. I love it in its own weird and wonderful way.

At *Hemmings Motor News*, it's our major promotion of the year. We have a presence in every field, we bring a lot of people to help. Of course, you have to be a lunatic like me to keep coming back and rummaging around year after year!

—*Dave Brownell*
Editor, Hemmings Motor News

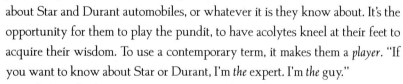

Contents

Something to Believe In

Go to Hershey, Pennsylvania, on the second weekend of October, and you'll see hundreds of thousands of people looking almost impossibly, effervescently *alive*. Their eyes

sparkle, their cheeks have a ruddy glow, they're enjoying themselves as only happy, excited pilgrims can enjoy themselves, knowing they're in the Center of the Universe. Their talk is a pleasant chatter, their heads swivel like radar dishes. It's the highpoint of the year for old car enthusiasts, and they're trying not to miss a thing.

THIS TOP-OF-THE-LINE '57 Pontiac Bonneville convertible sports a period license plate and spare tire "continental kit." What could be more evocative of Eisenhower Prosperity?

Old cars? All this excitement is about antique automobiles! These are wonderful old machines you can savor, get to know, enjoy and, yes—love. They're works of art that can take you way outside yourself to a special

BRASS ACETYLENE lamps and "cobra" bulbhorn were de rigueur for Pre-World War I sports and their Brass Era sports cars. Side marker lights like these are now prized collectibles worth $50 to $500 depending on condition. Acetylene lamps burn acetylene gas (HC-CH) produced when water and calcium carbide are combined in the lamp. They produce a surprisingly sharp, white light.

place in time. For many of us, this gilded past is an inviting escape from the overwhelming present.

If anything, this love of the past has gotten stronger in recent decades. As the world has become even more sterile, even more complex, even more controlled, the past looms as a time of excitement, of freedom, of heroic individualism. Social historians call this "soft primitivism," the natural human tendency to think everything was better back in the good ol' days.

But old cars are far more than simple escapism. Old cars are beloved as objects in themselves, for the purity of their lines, unencumbered by a wind tunnel engineer's concern for aerodynamics. Old cars are appealing because they are often simple enough that anyone can look at them and understand how they work. There is a directness, a sense of machinery, a *mechanicalness* that differentiates old cars from modern transportation modules.

Hershey fosters the appeal of old cars in many different ways. On the most superficial level, Hershey is nothing but an old car show, no different in principle from the annual Lion's Club car show at your local Little League field. To be specific, Hershey is the annual Antique Automobile Club of America's Eastern Division National Fall Meet, one of more than a dozen similar AACA meets held each year. You can examine a superbly restored group of antique cars and marvel at their looks, their sounds, the mechanical inventiveness of their builders, the artistry of their lines.

But Hershey is different. Unlike other AACA meets, around this nucleus of an old car show in a small Pennsylvania town a gathering has grown up, a happening that in its way is totally evocative of a happier, better time. One can go to Hershey and for four days in early October immerse yourself in a world in which nothing seems to have changed for 40 years.

Superficially defining Hershey is simple. There's an old car show, a swap meet where enthusiasts buy and sell parts for their old cars, a car corral where they buy and sell complete cars, an automobilia auction for car-related art and literature, a classic car exposition selling expensive collector machines. Plus, of course, there are all the unofficial activities that pop up anytime you put a quarter-of-a-million people in one place at one time, from barbecue dinners to an impromptu Dixieland band concert.

Since it started in the early-fifties, Hershey has grown from a handful of friends showing their cars to each other to 3,000 vendors and 2,000 exhibitors entertaining 250,000 spectators for four days. This makes Hershey not only the largest car show and swap meet in the world, it puts it right up there with the Indy 500, the Kentucky Derby and the Superbowl as an annual event at which record-breaking crowds converge. There is one important difference. Major sporting events celebrate the excellence of the present. Hershey celebrates the excellence of the past. To see a ninety-year-old car that looks better than new is to evoke the past through rose-tinted glasses.

Hershey also celebrates the promise of the future. To see a rusted hulk in the flea market that could—with the addition of thousands of dollars and years of work—be equally fine, is to hold out a tremendous hope. No one but an

EVERYONE SHARES some feeling of awe in the presence of a car in its fourth decade that looks like it was made yesterday. Witness the incredible detailing of this 1961 Chevrolet Impala Convertible.

optimist would even consider such a project, which means, by definition, Hershey attracts happy optimists with stars in their eyes.

It's this dual personality, of looking both to the past and to the future, that makes Hershey so unique. It has to do with truth. Old cars are machines, in the best sense of the word. Each part is crisp and functional, possessed of an innate beauty that only a well-engineered piece of metal can enjoy. Old cars are timeless, in the sense that their appeal is undiminished by the passage of years.

They are not just one-dimensional transportation, but a total aesthetic experience defined by excellence in engineering, design, color, texture, in everything that works together. Richard Wagner called an opera that held together aesthetically a *gesamkunstwerke*, and it's not too far fetched to apply the same term to an antique car.

I spend my days at Hershey in an ecstatic trance, caused by a sensory overload of looking, listening, smelling, driving and talking about old cars. These cars have more personality than many people I've met, for all that they are inanimate objects. To some people—myself included— this week is the most exciting thing they do all year, an experience, an interlude, an escape more precious than rubies. Hershey is the Center of the Universe for old-car enthusiasts, a spectacle that can't be missed. — *Rich Taylor*

Milton S. Hershey: a man unafraid to act on his dreams. He forever changed a small town in Central Pennsylvania into The Sweetest Place on Earth.

— **HERSHEY VISITOR'S GUIDE**

Chocolate Town, USA

The Hershey swap meet and car show takes place in Hershey, Pennsylvania, a company town built by Milton Hershey to house his world-famous chocolate factory and its attendant workers. Milton Snavely Hershey was born in a farmhouse in nearby Derry Church in 1857. His

Mennonite family is said to have originally emigrated from Switzerland. As a young man Hershey was apprenticed to a candy maker in Lancaster, but he soon moved to Philadelphia and, at 19, opened a candy shop. Ten years later, he returned to Lancaster and started the Lancaster Caramel Company.

SKOOTER, A 2-4-0 miniature 1907 locomotive, is one of the feature attractions at HersheyPark, a 90 acre amusement park adjacent to the car show.

In 1900, Hershey sold his successful caramel company for $1-million and moved back home to Derry Church. He acquired considerable land and in 1903 built what we would now call a greenfield factory in a nearby

LOOKING OUT ON THE swap meet field from Hershey Gardens, a 23 acre botanical garden near the Hershey Hotel.

UNIFORMED YOUNG women operate a high-tech chocolate bar wrapping machine in 1925. Hershey was already the largest chocolate factory in the world.

cornfield for the efficient production of fine milk chocolates. He also built a new town, Hershey, Pennsylvania, incorporating his birthplace of Derry Church. Why here? Aside from the fact that he'd grown up here, Hershey needed a constant supply of fresh milk. Central Pennsylvania was—and is—one of the premier milk producing areas in the United States, with acre upon acre of dairy farms within a day's drive by truck. For milk chocolate maker Milton Hershey, it was perfect.

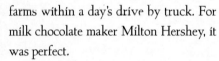

HERSHEY WAS ONE OF the first American companies to be mechanized, including a fleet of company-owned trucks to collect milk from nearby farms. This early chain-drive Mack was photographed in front of the corporate offices around 1910.

In 1907, Hershey came out with the famous Hershey Kiss, and Hershey Chocolate Company quickly grew into the largest chocolate manufacturing plant in the world. Today, Hershey produces 33 million kisses each day, some 12 billion annually. This rapid industrialization transformed what had been a pastoral farm area into a one-industry company town. Milton Hershey personally planned it as an ideal hometown for his workers. Hershey, Pennsylvania soon encompassed nearby Derry Church and filled the whole Spring Creek Valley.

Happily for the townspeople, Mr. Hershey grew philanthropic as he grew older, though like a Renaissance Medici, he obviously loved to see his name on as many buildings as possible. Among many other charitable gifts, he bought a large parcel of land along the Spring Creek and turned it into a public park, called of course, Hershey Park. In 1909, he started a school for homeless boys. The Milton Hershey School has since grown to an annual enrollment of 1,100 disadvantaged children.

In 1933, he spent $2-million to build the Hotel Hershey, giving employ-ment to 800 local craftsmen during its building and thousands more who've run the elegant resort over the six decades since. In the depths of the Great Depression, Mr. Hershey initiated a whole raft of other public buildings, too, sort of his own personal WPA intended to boost the local economy. Some, like the hotel, turned into profit centers. But the original impetus was a charitable one, very much in the spirit of Mr. Hershey's benign dictatorship which has now guided the Hershey area for the better part of a century.

Two years after building the hotel, elderly and childless, Mr. Hershey cre-ated the M.S. Hershey Foundation to provide an ongoing endowment for local education and cultural affairs. Among other things, the Hershey Foundation bankrolled the Milton S. Hershey Medical Center of Pennsylvania State Uni-versity. Since 1967, this has trained nearly 2,500 medical doctors.

Thanks to the generosity of Mr. Hershey and the philanthropists who fol-lowed him, Hershey, Pennsylvania has the aura of a park punctuated by spec-tacular tourist attractions. This is a real town, of course, but in many ways,

THE FOUNDATION OF A great American fortune, the Hershey factory has grown and grown for over a century. The landmark "Hershey Cocoa" hedge has welcomed visitors for decades.

Hershey, Pennsylvania is also an extension of the entertainment conglomerate now called Hershey Foods Corporation. The average small Pennsylvania farm community does not include a luxury hotel, a major medical school, a modern hotel/convention center, five golf courses, a botanical garden, an endowed school for needy children, a huge theatre/community center, an arena and stadium, a wildlife park, a riverside camp ground, a large corporate headquarters, a 100-acre amusement park and its own AHL hockey team. Plus, the largest chocolate factory in the world. No, it's not your average small town.

Hershey is clean, safe and prosperous, most people's idea of what a small town should be. There are tree-shaded streets lined with gracious older homes, there's an estate area where Hershey executives live, there's everything one could want, including a couple of above average restaurants and Harrisburg, the Pennsylvania state capitol, just a half-hour away. After a day or two, your nose gets used to the smell of milk chocolate and your stomach stops demanding a Hershey bar every hour on the hour. About then, you realize Hershey would be a pretty nice place to live.

The largest influx of visitors hits Hershey in October for the AACA car show and swap meet. Hotel rooms are sold out a year in advance—Hotel Hershey has a seven-year wait—but the rest of the town stays remarkably uncrowded. Why? Most of the hundreds of thousands of old car nuts never leave the swap meet. Except maybe to sleep. If you're a little more adventuresome—or you've already bought all the stuff your truck can hold—take a look around Milton Hershey's kingdom.

Start by driving up from the swap meet to Hershey Gardens, a hillside botanical garden which grew out of a rose garden begun by Milton's wife, Catherine Hershey. It now covers 23 acres. This is a lovely, quiet spot with a view over the whole car show/swap meet area. It's perfect for getting away from the crowds and taking a breather or getting an elevated view of treasures you may have overlooked.

ZooAmerica North American Wildlife Park, Hershey's 11-acre zoo, is an outgrowth of Mr. Hershey's private wild animal park. It's home to over 200 animals of 75 species, including bison, bear and eagles. The Milton Hershey homestead, Hershey Museum, Derry one-room school and Historical Derry Church are equally quiet and interesting. All are connected in some way with Milton Hershey, his

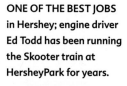

ONE OF THE BEST JOBS in Hershey; engine driver Ed Todd has been running the Skooter train at HersheyPark for years.

equivalent of Henry Ford Museum/Greenfield Village. If you're even more interested in the fascinating life of Milton Snavely Hershey, try Founders Hall at the Milton Hershey School. This houses the official version of the Milton Hershey story.

For more contemporary excitement—even though it's been there for 90 years—HersheyPark is the company-owned theme park. There's a brand new roller coaster, called the Wildcat, that covers two acres. HersheyPark also has a 1919 antique carousel that's a collector item in its own right plus Tidal Force, a splashdown ride for cooling off after a hot afternoon of slogging through swap meet dust. After that, you'll be ready for a visit to Hershey's Chocolate World where you'll be served up a free tour, a free chocolate bar and an ice cream soda that you'll have to pay for. Chocolate, of course.

SUNDAY AFTERNOON at Hershey Park, in the summer of 1915. Notice the cool open-air pavilions, the straw boaters on the men and immaculate white linen dresses of the women.

The Country Club of Hershey owns two public championship golf courses right near Hershey Park. Talk about nostalgia. Ben Hogan was the club professional for many years. Spring Creek Golf Course is right on Chocolate Avenue across the street from the Country Club. The Hotel Hershey offers yet more interesting golf.

Hershey also boasts more good places to eat than the national average for towns this size. Our favorite is Fenicci's, a low-key family-run Italian restaurant that's been on West Chocolate Avenue since 1935. Far fancier is the Circular Dining Room in the Hotel Hershey, the most upscale place to dine in the whole Hershey area.

The Hotel Hershey is also totally unexpected in a small town, an AAA Four Diamond Grand Hotel comparable in some ways to The Greenbrier, The Balsams and other classic American resorts. It's not even terribly expensive for what you get. The Hotel Hershey offers very traditional amusements. Lawn bowling, carriage rides and tea on the terrace are prime afternoon treats. You don't even have to close your eyes to pretend it's 1935 all over again.

IT'S TRUE, THE STREET lamps in Hershey really are shaped like Hershey's Kisses. They were first installed in 1961.

THE HERSHEY FACTORY in 1920, with rush hour traffic along Chocolate Avenue and street cars waiting to pick up the overflow. Notice the wonderfully evocative turn-of-the-century architecture, showing a lot of plate glass—very modern in its day.

TOPIARY KISSES LINE the downtown area, repeating forms that constantly remind you where you are. Hershey is really "the town that kisses built." Introduced in 1907, the chocolate kiss provided the foundation for Hershey's fortunes. Today, Hershey plants in Hershey, Pennsylvania and Oakdale, California produce 33 million kisses per day, a whopping 12 billion kisses each year.

Old car nuts are usually keen on anything mechanical that moves under its own power. In addition to the miniature railroad at HersheyPark, there's the nearby Middletown & Hummelstown Railroad, which runs excursions in antique rail cars. If you're a historian, the Civil War battlefield of Gettysburg is just a short drive, as are the quaint cities of Lancaster and York.

Got a day or two to spend after Hershey? Wander the lovely back roads of this Pennsylvania Dutch countryside, unchanged since the early nineteenth century. Picturesque barns, stone houses and perfectly tended farms provide their own varied adventures to modern travelers. In your concentration on the old car portion of Hershey, be sure not to miss the complete experience.

Keepers of the Flame

The Antique Automobile Club of America was begun by a group of 14 car enthusiasts in Philadelphia, and chartered in November of 1935. Since then, it has grown steadily to today's nearly 60,000 members. In addition to car shows across the country and many local tours, the AACA organizes the Revival Glidden Tour, a rally that commemorates the long-distance reliability contests organized by automotive pioneer Charles J. Glidden beginning in 1905.

HERSHEY, 1967: 1903 Curved-Dash Oldsmobile getting toweled-down before judging. Preserving Brass Era cars like this is why the AACA was originally formed.

One important decision distinguishes the AACA from most other old car groups. Most clubs are frozen in time, in that they collect Model A Fords, or '55-'57 Chevies or Shelby-built Mustangs. The AACA decided years ago that any vehicle at least

HERSHEY, 1968: This 1932 Oldsmobile L-32 Eight displays dozens of AACA National event participation plaques.

HERSHEY, 1960: THE CAR that started it all, Henry Ford's 1903 Model A, with two-cylinder engine under the seat. Cars like this formed the backbone of the AACA for decades. Notice that the Hershey car show had already outgrown its original site inside the stadium; some cars were displayed inside, some outside on the adjacent practice field. You can see the outside of the stadium behind these ladies.

25 years old is an antique, deserves preservation, and thus can be shown at AACA shows. Each year, in other words, a new group of cars becomes eligible for AACA competition.

The AACA should really be called the Antique Vehicle Club of America. They define "automobile" to include not only old passenger cars, but racing cars, motorcycles, Whizzer motorbikes, trucks, buses and even such off-beat machines as a Volkswagen pickup truck fitted with a hydraulic bucket lift that often shows up at the Hershey car show.

All of this means that each year the AACA not only opens itself to new and interesting vehicles, but new and interesting members, as well. It's all extremely healthy, because without new, younger and more varied members, the club would literally die off. There are almost no members left who can remember lusting after Pre-World War I Brass Era cars as a teenager, and the prices and appreciation of these cars have declined while enthusiasm among Baby Boomers for the '65 Mustangs and '67 Camaros they remember as teenagers has boomed. The AACA was one of the first groups—and still the largest and most important—to recognize that change in the old car ranks is a positive force.

AACA's membership is divided into hundreds of semi-autonomous regions and chapters, some with as few as fifteen members. Each region or chapter can organize its own events and meetings. As you might expect, the Hershey Region is one of the largest and most enthusiastic, with over 500 members who work in their spare time year-round preparing for their one stupendous weekend in early October.

Hershey is only one of a dozen AACA National meets each year. These events take place all over the United States and are spread throughout the year.

This year, for example, there were February Nationals in Philadelphia, Pennsylvania and Plantation, Florida, an April National in Dallas, Texas, May Nationals in Indian Wells, California and Kingsport, Tennessee, June Nationals in Johnstown, Pennsylvania and Dearborn, Michigan, a July National in Akron, Ohio, an August National in Grand Forks, North Dakota, September Nationals in Chesapeake, Virginia and Tucson, Arizona, the October National at Hershey, Pennsylvania and a November National in Jacksonville, Florida. The annual Grand National was in Huntsville, Alabama in mid-July. This schedule changes somewhat each year, with events hosted by different AACA regions that volunteer to put on an event.

Hershey, of course, being by far the biggest and most popular AACA National, has a life of its own. Indeed, there are probably thousands of old car buffs who think the AACA's only activity is to host Hershey. Having the national headquarters in Hershey just compounds that confusion. The truth, of course, is that the AACA is an especially vibrant and constantly growing organization, the largest old car club in the world, with members all over the United States and most foreign countries. Even if you took away the Hershey weekend, the AACA would still be a major force in the old car hobby. Including Hershey, the AACA is the most important old car organization in America.

AACA HEADQUARTERS is in this pleasant old building west of town near the Hershey Lodge, right on Route 322. It used to be a dormitory for the Milton Hershey School.

When I started coming here in 1965, we used to park in the middle of the Blue Field and walk to the flea market. We'd be blown away by the enormity of it all. Prewar and Brass Era cars were shown inside the stadium. Every Friday, they'd demonstrate race cars on the stadium track, not racing, but driving around. You'd see some just wonderful cars.

— **JOHN PAULDING**

Origins Of Greatness

From 1950 to 1952, there was an annual old car show in Devon, Pennsylvania, at the old Devon horse ring. It was attended by no more than a handful of old car nuts. In 1953, the Devon show was moved to nearby Hershey.

HERSHEY, 1967: EVEN IN the old days, it wasn't strictly old cars. This early Wurlitzer Band Organ drew an admiring crowd of listeners in the display field.

And thus is immortality born.

It was run by the National AACA, this first Hershey show, since the Hershey Region hadn't even begun at that time. Old-timers remember it as having twelve cars on display.

By 1955, the newly chartered Hershey Region put on its first car show in the Hershey Stadium over the weekend of October eighth and ninth. Less than twenty local old-car owners showed up. There was no flea market to speak of, just half-a-dozen people selling parts.

HERSHEY, 1967: AUTO-
mobilia is nothing new—
their sons are still trading
the same old license
plates today.

HERSHEY, 1970: THE cars on display are Brass Era cars, at least some of which you might still see at Hershey today. They're shown at one end of the football field inside the Hershey stadium. Notice the goal post in amongst the cars.

By 1956, there were still only two dozen cars and a few people selling parts. Back then, of course, the AACA numbered only a few thousand members and there weren't 100,000 people in the whole world who thought of themselves as old-car collectors. But the boom had started.

By 1958, there were 300 cars in the show. By 1963, *Automobile Quarterly* was able to report in pleased amazement that the Hershey car show attracted 600 entries and 20,000 spectators who came to ogle Mercers, Stanley Steamers and Isotta Fraschinis as well as the more mundane Model Ts and Buicks on display. Cars from before 1915—what collectors call Brass Era cars—were most in demand, with an emphasis on cars like the Eldredge, Baker or Dagmar whose names are now unfamiliar even to die-hard old car buffs. The AACA now totalled 16,000 members who owned 20,000 pre-1935 cars.

Many of these cars were owned by men whose names have since become

FOR 40 YEARS

I've been coming to Hershey every year since 1955. The first year I came, there were 12 cars and no flea market at all. The next year, we had 20 cars and maybe three flea market vendors at the swap meet. The whole show was inside the stadium. In 40 years, it's grown into what you see now. We have 2,000 cars and trucks in the show, and another 1,700 for sale in the car corral.

I think this may be the last year I do this. It's always been my hobby, always just for fun. But I had a big fire and lost a lot of my stuff. I restored a '22 Cleveland that went in the fire, and a '41 Packard. But I've done the Glidden Tour, done a lot of other things, had a lot of fun in this hobby over the past 40 years.

—*Holly Carlson*
Swap Meet Vendor

HERSHEY, 1970: IT seemed huge at the time, but the entire car show fit inside the stadium. This is looking west where cars from the twenties and thirties were parked. Hershey School overlooks the grounds, just as it does today.

legendary in the old car hobby: Henry Austin Clark, Jr., D. Cameron Peck, Dr. Samuel Scher, Richard Riegel, Jr., William Harrah, Briggs Cunningham, Jack Frost, George Waterman. They—and thousands of other less well-known collectors—saved the cars which still provide the backbone of the old car hobby. Add the paintings of Peter Helck and Walter Gotschke, the books of Ken Purdy and Ralph Stein, and you have the basis of today's explosion of interest.

Even in the early-sixties, American antique car enthusiasts still thought it was cute to dress up in old clothing that they fondly imagined matched the period of their car. As Ralph Stein wrote in 1961, "It is still de rigueur for women to wear plumed hats and lace dresses, while the men appear in top hats (to which are affixed goggles), string ties, violently checked tail coats, and spats. If you showed up at a British meet looking like that, they'd chuck you into the Thames."

By 1970, the funny clothes were gone, replaced by bell-bottoms and leather vests, another generation's idea of style which today looks more dated than the straw boaters and blazers that our great-grandfathers wore. Hershey Weekend had exploded from a one-day event to a swap meet that began on Friday, with a car show on Saturday. In 1970, there were 1,083 swap meet vendors and 912 vehicles in the show, according to Hershey Region records.

Ten years later, there were 5,500 vendor spaces and 1,067 cars to be judged. In 1989, at the height of the old car boom, there were 2,000 cars in the car show and 3,000 vendors renting 10,000 vendor spaces. That enthusiasm has continued into the nineties. In 1996, for example, 3,300 vendors occupied 10,000 vendor spaces. There were 1,900 cars in the show and another 1,800 for sale in the car corral. Around 250,000 spectators attended, encouraged no doubt by lack of an admission charge. No other old car meet in the world even approaches these figures.

How big has the old car hobby become? Well, according to Bob Pass of Passport Transport, there are at least 200 tractor-trailer rigs kept busy full-time

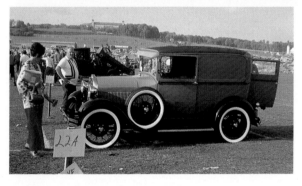

TIMELESS HERSHEY:
Photos taken by Russ von Sauers in the late-sixties/early-seventies are tough to distinguish from those taken thirty years later. (Clockwise from top left) A rare Alfa Romeo 1750, a coffin-nose '37 Cord, a single-seat oval track racer from the twenties, a '48 Lincoln Continental, the track racer again and a Model A Sedan Delivery. Any one of these cars would be a star at Hershey today.

(ABOVE) PHOTOGRAPHER
Russ von Sauers grabs yet
another shot at a recent
Hershey car show.

just moving old cars from one concours to another, from one restoration shop to another, from one garage to another. The experts claim there are now roughly 10 million people in America alone who own some sort of collector car. Over 3 million of them consider "collecting old cars" to be their primary hobby. With this kind of growth, it's no wonder that the Hershey car show and swap meet has grown exponentially, too.

As most car enthusiasts know, there was a tremendous boom in old car prices and enthusiasm in the eighties, followed by a bust in 1988 and '89. The good news is that the increased enthusiasm is still with us, but old car prices have come back down to a level that normal folks can pay. A lot of speculators may have lost a lot of money in the crash, but the average old car collector is better off. This is why there are more and more exhibitors and enthusiasts at Hershey; they can afford to be here.

Since the late-fifties, Hershey has been the largest car show and swap meet in the world. The difference is that back then, Hershey was the *only* event of its

REMEMBERING THE HERSHEY CAR SHOW

I can remember my father, Kenneth Mayes, bringing his 1911 Franklin Touring Car to the AACA Eastern meet at Hershey in the fifties. Hershey was nothing like it is now, of course, but it seemed immense back then. But what I remember most about Hershey has to do with our own cars, not with the show itself. We were so intent on doing well in the judging. I guess we didn't know any better!

We didn't own a trailer, and it was too far to drive, so we towed the Franklin down there with a tow bar, as I recall. Since then, I've spent much of my life around men taking race cars to different places, and I've learned that a tow bar is about the worst way to move a car!

The first thing we did when we hit town was to wash the car; it had to be immaculate. I remember spending a lot of time polishing brass and wiping the paint down. We were very proud of our Franklin. My father won a Junior Second, and I remember he was disappointed at not winning. But honestly, it was probably not a first-place car. He hadn't spent all that much money on it, and by that time, even back in the mid-fifties, people were already doing expensive, full-house restorations.

Then my father and a friend of his found a 1931 duPont Model H in a wood lot in Virginia and did a complete restoration. This was a beautiful car, a dual-cowl phaeton with a sweeping paint job like a Duesenberg. It was black and white, with a swept-back windshield and dual driving lights. It was the neatest car, absolutely gorgeous.

It nearly won Best of Show at Hershey. My father then sold the duPont to the Thompson Museum, then it went to Richard Riegel, Jr. who was part of the duPont family. There was a jigsaw puzzle made of it, and it's featured in a 1963 *Automobile Quarterly*. I even did an article about it for *Road & Track*. The duPont was a wonderful car and a big part of my Hershey memories.

—*Sandra Leitzinger*
Automotive Artist

kind. People were already showing classics on the lawn at Pebble Beach, and there were other local shows. But Hershey was the first meet to attract people from not only around the country, but from all over the world.

Today, Chip and Bill Miller's Fall Carlisle show is very popular, plus there's Spring Carlisle, Spring Hershey, the Pomona swap meets and literally hundreds of other swap meets and car shows around the country. Hershey covers 182 acres, and at the moment, it's still the biggest and the best. But the Hershey Region turns away thousands of swap meet applicants each year, so it could be bigger and better still.

In the time-honored tradition of Hershey, perhaps it's time to expand again. They could easily move the parking areas further away, and establish a whole new field—maybe two—that would handle growth for the foreseeable future. Imagine Hershey with 50 percent more vendors! It'd take a week to see everything, if you hurried along.

Of course, thirty years ago, people said if Hershey got any bigger, they'd never be able to cover it all. Since then, Hershey has tripled in area, the car show has doubled its numbers, and the spectators have increased ten times over. But somehow, everybody still finds time to cover it all. Well, most of it, anyway! No doubt they'll still manage in the future, no matter how big Hershey becomes.

HERSHEY, 1972: AS YOU can see from this aerial shot, even three decades ago, the swap meet and car show were still quite small. What's now the White Field was Hershey Airport, visible in the upper right corner of this photo, just below Hershey School. What used to be the primary swap meet area is now used for trailer parking. Spectators parked in today's Green Field and Chocolate Field.

My son takes the week off from school to help me set up, my wife comes and helps me run the booth. For us, Hershey is an annual family outing. We've been doing it so long, we can put up a tent and lay out our parts in a couple of hours. We can pack up even faster.

— **MORT PAPPAS**

Overnight Encampment

It's like one of those huge Civil War set piece battles. Like Gettysburg, maybe. Robert E. Lee looks out from the woods and there are a few blue jackets on top of the hill across the way. No problem. He wakes up the next morning, and the entire Army of the Potomac has moved in, 80,000 Yankees staring down their gun barrels at his long white beard.

Hershey is like that. One minute there's nothing much here, just an empty field, a tired old football stadium and two guys slowly unrolling snow fencing at the edge of the road. The next morning there are 250,000 people spread over 182 acres, camping on the grass with enough motorhomes, trailers and trucks to house most of Philadelphia. At least they're friendly.

HOW MANY FLEA marketers does it take to snap open a canopy? As many as there are. One thing about Hershey, everybody wants to help.

PROBABLY CARPENTERS at home, some guys build as though they're planning to stay for years, not just four days. Bet he couldn't get away with using a board and a screw jack instead of a hammer at his day job.

BEFORE MR. HERSHEY built a factory in a cornfield, most of the countryside around Derry Church looked like this; peaceful Mennonite dairy farms, neat as a pin, with big houses and even bigger, white-washed barns. The "Pennsylvania Dutch"—actually farmers from Germany and German-speaking Switzerland—settled this area in the early 19th century.

Swap meet spaces, of course, must be reserved from the Hershey Region in advance. Each 10x30 foot space costs only $51 for the week, one of the greatest business bargains in the world. Most spaces are held by the same person or company for decades, though about 500 of the 10,000 available change hands each year. People have actually bequeathed Hershey swap meet spaces to their children or grandchildren, and the Hershey Region AACA honors these bequests.

Hershey starts on a Tuesday. Well, *really* it starts on a Thursday the week before that, when a whole bunch of the same vendors and spectators show up at Carlisle Fairgrounds for Fall Carlisle. Fall Carlisle is the same kind of thing, a swap meet and car corral, but aimed more at post-war cars. The serious swap meet buyers and sellers start their autumn season at Carlisle. Of course, there

HERSHEY LOCALS DO an amazing job of handling traffic that would daunt Disneyland or Las Vegas. Directing traffic is just a minor part of transporting, feeding, sheltering and cleaning hundreds of thousands of visitors.

are also those guys who go to Carlisle, sell off a pile of stuff, then find some other incredible bargain that they can turn around at Hershey for a profit. Buy, sell, trade. It becomes a way of life.

It's only about an hour drive from Carlisle to Hershey, so every year Hershey starts sooner as more people arrive early to get the jump on the crowds. Tuesday morning at 10 A.M., there are already some advance scouts in place. On Wednesday comes the deluge; the car corral opens at 7 A.M., the flea market at 10 A.M. After that, until Sunday morning, it's every man for himself.

One of the things that's unique about Hershey is its diversity. People come from all over the country and all over the world, it's true. But more importantly, they have varying ideas about what to bring and sell, what's the appropriate dress for a flea market in the mud, what's comfortable lodging, what's effective display, what's protective shelter. You see this most clearly during the set-up.

First, you have your professional or semi-professional flea market vendors.

These folks own elaborate trailers with sides that swing up to form roofs over counters that display the merchandise. It takes them just half-an-hour to set up, because everything is already in place from Carlisle. Then there are the experienced vendors who've been coming here for decades, but who can't justify the expense of a custom-built trailer. They have pop-up tents or canopies that unroll from the side of a motorhome. Everything is pre-labelled and priced and needs only to be grouped on tables under the tent. These are the people who recruit a few friends for the weekend, knowing it's almost impossible to do everything yourself, even setting up and taking down the display.

Then there are the folks who've never done this before. They either spread a bunch of unlabelled parts and delicate literature directly on the grass, unprotected from the rain and sun, or buy stacks of 2 x 4s at the local lumberyard and build a wild tarp-covered structure big enough to house a Civil War battalion. They hammer out built-in shelves, cabinets—even home-built shower stalls—everything but the kitchen sink. Just about the time they put the last finishing touches on their architectural wonder, it's time to take it all apart again and head back home.

HIGH HOPES AND NEAT cars: this guy plans to sell his '57 Mercury and '54 Chevy at the car corral. Both have period accessories. Check out the visor on the Chevy and the cruiser skirts on the salmon and white Monterey.

ERSHEYPARK STADIUM

.M.   SEPT. 30

HERSHEY
MUSE

EARLY BIRDS HEADING for the swap meet area where they just know they'll find what they're looking for.

You see funny things going on at Hershey all the time. There used to be a guy who wore a hubcap strapped on his head. Mr. Hubcap. Haven't seen him in a while. Wonder what happened to Mr. Hubcap?

— **AL WILSON**

Where Do They Find This Stuff?

Ahrens-Fox. Allard. Alternators/Generators. Alvis. Ambulance/Fire Service. AMC/AMX. American LaFrance. American Underslung.

YOUR LOW-BUCK SWAP meet display—milk crates full of parts laid on the ground. Ah, but in this case, the parts are rare antique fire hose nozzles that somebody *needs*.

These are just some of the entries on the first page of the Hershey Region's list of flea market vendors, arranged by speciality. Thirty pages later, the list winds up with Velie, Whizzer, Willys, Willys Knight and Willys Overland. Somewhere between Ahrens-Fox and Willys Overland, there's something for everyone. The hard part is finding it in Hershey's 182 acres and 10,300 flea market spaces.

It would be easier if the Hershey Region would group vendors by specialty, putting all the Model T guys cheek by jowl, for example, instead of having everyone

THIS GRILLE FROM A 1938 Hudson Terraplane transcends "rusty old car part" to become a handsome work of art.

A 1932 CADILLAC V-12
produces 135 HP @ 3400
rpm from a 368 cubic inch

mixed up all higglety-pigglety. But the AACA respects nothing so much as tradition. There are flea market vendors who've had the same swap meet spaces for three decades; their friends and customers wouldn't know where to find them if there was some logical grouping. Indeed, Hershey Region did move some vendors around a few years ago and caused an outcry that still hasn't abated. Until some iron-willed organizer takes over and forces everyone to change, Hershey will keep its charmingly haphazard layout.

It's easy to figure out the interests of the Hershey crowd just from the swap meet listings. Last year there were only seven vendors dealing in parts for European Sports Cars, but 250 separate companies and individuals selling parts for Model A Fords. That's not counting the hundreds of other names listed under other Ford models, or the hundreds more listed as Ford, FoMoCo, etc. Or the sign sellers who have Ford tin signs, etc. Other things may change, cars may come and go out of popularity, but the heart of Hershey is still prewar Ford.

At the same time, the variety of artifacts spread over Hershey's lawns is truly formidable. In a single swap meet space you might see a Tokheim gas pump, a rack of Texaco oil cans, a Schwinn Excelsior bicycle, water pumps for a 59 AB Ford and taillights for a 1960 Chrysler. Not to mention cubic yards of parts that only the man who needs that particular part can identify. Multiply this cornucopia of stuff by Hershey's 10,000 swap meet spaces, and you begin to understand the magnitude of the task that faces any Hershey shopper. Nobody knows how many separate items there are, but three to four million is probably a pretty conservative guesstimate.

I'm sure there are people who come to Hershey and methodically see everything in every space, all four million items, people who start at the westernmost point of the Green Field and sweep back and forth until they reach the stadium, examining everything there is to examine. Of course, by the time they get to the other end, half the stuff has been sold, but in theory, a very strong-willed person could do Hershey in an organized and proper manner.

OLD ENAMELED TIN signs, not just auto related, fill this vendor's tent. There's enough here to decorate a whole theme restaurant.

I always vow to be organized, but I always get distracted within the first hour and end up for the rest of the weekend running hither and yon to see whatever bright and shiny gee-gaw attracts me most strongly at that instant. And then, having barely satisfied myself with that delight, I'm off to find the next irresistible exotica.

In addition to parts and cars, mostly what one finds at Hershey is information. Watch the people at

LITERATURE, MODELS, promotional models still in the original boxes, new models cashing in on the model collecting craze, car toys, NOS parts still in mint packaging. There are a lot of things to look at and think about just in this one tent. And Hershey has 3,200 tents.

Hershey as you wander around the swap meet. What are they doing? Talking. The old car hobby is filled with the darnedest group of talkers, chatterers, questioners, story-tellers, *raconteurs*, that you'd ever want to see.

Look around. The whole place is abuzz with the low murmur of conversation. This is true of every old car group, every old car event I've been to in the past forty years. They're the talkingest group of people you'd ever want to meet. Nobody can make a decision without talking it over with everyone in sight,

NOS

I'm a carpenter from Barnard, Vermont. Two years ago I bought a whole garage from the widow of a guy who repaired cars from the twenties up through the sixties. I got all these original parts in the original boxes. Because he was in Vermont, he repaired tractors and trucks and Jeeps, primarily. So the parts are very different from the ordinary flea market parts.

Everything is NOS [New Old Stock], in the original boxes. I've gone through every part and indexed it against old books, so I know what vehicle each part fits. That

makes the parts more valuable. The rarest parts were sold last year—I had Cadillac and Packard and Reo parts—so now I'm just trying to clean out all the rest.

I collect old Chevrolets, so I kept all the Chevrolet parts for myself. I think that's pretty typical of a lot of people here. They sell stuff to support their own cars, so it doesn't end up costing them a lot of money to own old cars. For most of us, Hershey is also our annual vacation.

—*Glenn Feeney*
Swap Meet Vendor

AMONG THE BIGGEST draws at Hershey are the acres and acres of NOS parts, parts for any car under the sun. If you can't find it here, you can't find it anywhere.

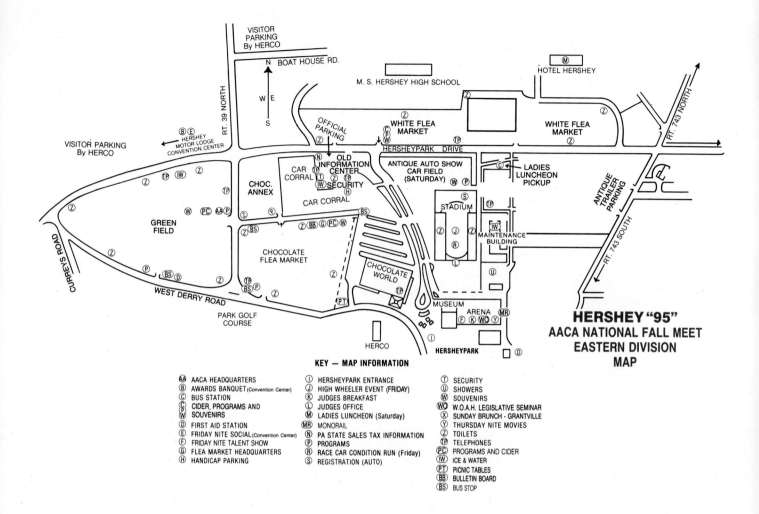

OVER THE YEARS, Hershey has grown out of all recognition. At the beginning, the whole show took place in the stadium. By the sixties, the swap meet was in the Blue Field, what's now all amusements, with the car show in the stadium and adjacent practice field. Since then, the Green Field, Chocolate Field and White Field have been added, plus the car corral in the Chocolate Annex. It's a good four times larger than in 1970, and it seemed immense then.

examining the problem from every possible point of view. It's like being part of a Jane Austen novel or a big family where every decision is made by a consensus that always includes all the kids.

Why does this happen? Because the whole point of the old car hobby is interacting with other enthusiasts, sharing information, sharing sources, sharing ideas. Most old cars enthusiasts have very few friends or neighbors who share their interest. So coming to Hershey is, in a very real sense, a reaffirmation of faith, a chance to reconfirm that they aren't the only ones wandering in the wilderness. It's nice to know there are people who understand when you start dribbling on about some incredibly arcane old car topic, like the Miller jet-bar carburetor or the proper diameter of coolant flow restrictors for a Ford V-8.

More than nice, it's important. Let's pose a hypothetical problem, but one that is very real. Your Ford flathead V-8 is overheating. You've read the books by Ron Bishop and Bill Sinclair, you've made all their recommended changes, and still your flathead overheats. What do you do next? You come to Hershey, where there are literally hundreds of experts on the flathead Ford, and you talk to everyone you can find. And more than likely, they'll know how to solve your problem because they've seen it and cured it before. Hershey isn't just about old cars and old parts, Hershey is about knowledge.

Some buyers come with a wish list, match that up with the list of vendors, and seek out the particular sellers who most likely will have what they need. If you admit that Hershey is just too big for any one person to see in four days, this probably makes the most sense. At least you see what you're interested in.

But half the fun of Hershey is in seeing things that are all new to you, that you didn't know existed or that you'd forgotten about. And the way you do that is to arrive with no preconceived plan, other than to wander around and see what looks intriguing. Realistically, you can see one field—Green, White, Chocolate—in a day. Plus, you can easily spend a whole afternoon dreaming at the car corral and another half-day at the Saturday car show. If you do it right, you'll either meet old friends or make new friends, then go see some special something that they've discovered and you wouldn't know about unless you'd met them. With a little luck, it might even be a part you've been looking for.

UP WITH THE DAWN, this serious shopper is looking for early bargains. Note the Little Red Wagon for hauling parts back to the pickup truck.

Unexpected things do happen. For example, I went to Hershey one year looking for speed parts for my Allard race car, which while it's as British as a Cornish Pasty, has a Ford flathead V-8 under the hood. I walked in the gate of the Chocolate Field and saved myself $4,500. Bargain Ford parts? Nope. Something totally unexpected.

You see, back home in the barn I have a 1961 Norton Dominator 88 motorcycle. The kid who works in the local garage wanted it in the worst way. I was about to let him buy it for $500. But there, in the first swap meet booth I came to was a virtually identical Norton Domi 88 with a $5,000 pricetag. And plastered under the price was a sticker that read "Sold." I was $4,500 ahead on the day and I hadn't even found a cup of coffee yet. Good things like that happen all the time at Hershey.

The professional swap meet shoppers—and there are plenty of those—are here to snatch up bargains, then turn them over at a higher price to someone else. This requires a couple of things. You've got to be the first one on the field at dawn, you've got to know exactly what any item is worth, you've got to have cash to buy it and most important of all, you've got to be able to make a quick decision before someone else comes along and grabs your bargain out from under your nose.

You can tell the pros. They're the ones with cellular phones so they can confer with their partners who're working other parts of the field or check-in with clients back home to make sure they really want that Model A carburetor, even for $2,000. The pro shoppers find a good buy, confirm by phone and plunk down the greenbacks they just obtained from the ATM.

BUYING AND SELLING PARTS

We sell parts and miscellaneous stuff at Hershey. The fun of it is, you go around to swap meets across the country and if you see something interesting, you buy it. Then a couple of years later, you bring it to Hershey and sell it. It's strictly a hobby, just for fun. Back home in Michigan, I'm a bricklayer by trade.

I went out to dinner with a couple of guys last night and they'd just bought cars here. One of them bought a big Packard, the other one bought a Mercedes. I'm looking for Minerva parts, myself. They're so rare. I have half-a-

dozen old cars that I drive; a couple of Minervas, a 1937 Daimler. At Hershey, it's hard to find parts because everything is all jumbled up. Mustang parts are next to Cadillac parts are next to Mercedes parts. You never know what you'll find.

Twenty years ago Hershey was a lot smaller. They had a little bit of a car corral, maybe 20 or 30 cars. Today, I can't count how many cars are here.

—*Ed DeGrace*
Swap Meet Vendor

"ONE MAN'S JUNK IS another man's treasure." No doubt, somewhere there's somebody desperate for rusted old cigarette machines.

Like any swap meet, Hershey is strictly cash only. I learned my lesson years ago. I came to buy some Corvette parts and there in the car corral was an absolutely perfect Porsche 911 for $6,500. It was easily worth $10,000 at the time. I offered $1,000 in cash that I had in my pocket, a check for $5,500 and I'd drive the owner and his wife to their home an hour away. Another buyer walked up as I was explaining all this, whipped out five $1,000 bills and bought the car on the spot. The owner said it wasn't that he didn't trust me, but he'd rather have $5,000 in cash and take a taxi home than $6,500 tomorrow, when the bank opened.

What's it like to be a swap meet vendor? Well, you stand around and talk to people, just like being a swap meet buyer. Even better, people hand you money instead of you paying out. The downside is that people expect you to know what you're talking about, since you're the "expert." There's no heavier burden.

Rene Dreyfus, the famous French racing driver and owner of Le Chanteclair restaurant in Manhattan, used to say, "I don't have to travel anywhere. If I stay here, pretty soon everyone will come to visit *me*." Running a swap meet space is like that. Pretty soon, everybody you want to see will find you, as well as a couple of guys you didn't even know you needed to meet. Of course, you also

IT ONLY SEEMS LIKE rust is the most popular color at Hershey. These early Ford parts are going to make somebody's day.

"READY FOR WORK OR Play, 1962 Chevrolet Stepside Pickup, Used as parts-getter at Cardamone's Garage. Well-rusted, seriously abused by a long string of teenage helpers. Needs everything. Best offer or tow it away. Trailer available. Inquire within."

IT MAY LOOK ROUGH to you, but this nose from a 1935 Ford truck will be just what some restorer has been searching for.

want to check out the competition, which is a good argument to bring a couple of helpers with you, somebody who can man the store when you're not there.

What sells at Hershey? Anything and everything. Stuff you'd think anyone would covet and stuff you'd think you couldn't give away. If I had any advice to give to a swap meet vendor, I'd say bring stuff you haven't been able to sell anywhere else, the stranger the better. Hershey is where that one guy who needs whatever it is will find you.

Obviously, the better the quality the easier the sale, but there's an interesting quirk to the psyche of the old car enthusiast. Most people, offered a perfect car radio for $50 or a broken one for $30, will take the working radio, even though it costs more. The old car enthusiast, on the other hand, will always choose the broken radio, on the theory that he'll have fun fixing it and save $20, besides. Of course, it will cost $100 to repair, but he doesn't count that part.

Where do people find this stuff? In their barns. I walked through my buddy Kurt Vaughn's barn the other day. He's got a stack of early Mustang parts left over from a '66 convertible restoration. There's a bunch of big block Ford stuff left over from another project, a race-prepped C-4 transmission, a set of NOS 1968 Trans-Am racing tires that came on a set of wheels that I bought from him and redrilled to put on my Corvette, a complete '48 Ford front suspension, a Crosley Super Sport that needs a total restoration, all the side trim off a Mercedes 300. Stuff just accumulates. After a while, you have to clear it out in order to gain room for the next project. So every year, Kurt bundles it all into a truck and brings it to Hershey. All this stuff that's become a burden to him is going to save the day for somebody else. "One man's junk is another man's treasure" is never more true than at the Hershey swap meet.

Guys like Kurt epitomize the Hershey vendor, individual collectors simultaneously cleaning out their barns and helping their fellow collectors find stuff

MR. CROSLEY

Why do we all come to Hershey? To meet our friends with whom we correspond over the year. To look for parts, to see cars we've heard about, to explore new cars and areas of interest. It's nice to find out who's reproducing parts, who's doing what. Even the parade of cars on the highways when you go out for dinner is interesting.

You meet a lot of really nice people, you have fun talking to people, you learn a lot. You can help other people. I met a man today and I was able to identify a part for him that he'd been scratching his head about. That's rewarding. To be honest, I don't come for the food!

I own a marketing research company in Montreal, and this is my fourth Hershey. The first year, I came with a friend to see what it was all about. The second year, I came looking for parts for a Crosley I was restoring. The third time, I brought the restored car and got a Junior First. This year, I paid my $75 for a

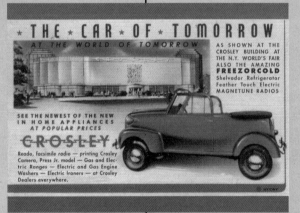

spot in the car corral and came back to sell the car, which will finance my next project, a Crosley Hot Shot.

There's a huge change taking place in the old car hobby right now. There's a large group that's dying off. The early cars that they have will have to be passed on to younger people. Luckily, the 30-year-olds who own Mustangs and Camaros will eventually get interested in older cars. The more experience you have in the hobby, the more your tastes broaden and the more interest you have in the older cars. But if we don't educate the kids about these cars, the hobby won't survive.

Luckily, I'm from Canada where old cars are seen as part of our national heritage. But we have to come down to Hershey to find rust-free, Southern cars.

—*Robert Head*
Car Corral Vendor

A TREASURE TROVE OF
hard to find chrome and
lenses, mostly Chrysler.

ORGANIZING HERSHEY

Normally, the way the AACA works is that a region applies for a meet, and the AACA allows a different region to host its various National or Grand National meets each year. Hershey is unique, in that it is the only AACA National that doesn't move around. In the early days, it just happened that way, and now, it's become sort of an institution. It probably helps that the AACA National Headquarters is here, too.

Hershey Week is really a collaboration between Herco and the Hershey Region of the AACA. Herco is the company that controls the property once owned by Milton Hershey, I'd say they own thousands of acres in and around Hershey. The Hershey Region rents the land from Herco for the week. We also rent the use of the Stadium and any other facilities. We pay Herco to put up snow fencing for crowd control, and we pay for auxiliary police. We pay for stone to fill mud holes if it rains, and we even have to pay to tow vendors' vehicles out of the fields if they get stuck.

We give Herco 50 spaces for food stands. Herco controls all food; they subcontract the spaces out to hot-dog vendors, or pizza vendors, or whatever. The only thing that Hershey Region is allowed to sell are the famous apples and cider, plus our programs and souvenirs, and that's all by donation. Herco also controls all the parking, both for motorhomes and daily car parking.

We have 500 members of the Hershey Region; we had to cut it off because we didn't have a place large enough for us all to meet. We try to keep our members from within a 50 mile radius of Hershey. Including their families and friends, we'll get over 700 volunteers to run the show. Volunteers do everything from parking cars to laying out the swap meet field.

We do everything with volunteers. We have to lay out the fields; every space is marked with a numbered tag with the vendor's name. It takes one whole Sunday to lay out the flea market, the weekend before the event. We get a big group of volunteers, and we just do it.

We start working on it between Christmas and New Year; that's when we send out all the pre-registrations for flea market spaces. Everyone who was there last year gets first choice for next year. You can keep your same spaces, no more, though you can give up a space if you want to. You can even will your space to someone else. If somebody dies, and their son or daughter wants the space, we'll give it to them. It's almost like a family.

By March, all that paperwork starts coming back. Usually, there are about 500 vendor spaces which change hands, usually in the outlying fields. I bet there aren't 20 spaces that change hands in the Chocolate Field. We have to turn away many more people who want to sign up. We could probably sell 500 more spaces.

Those available spaces are noted in the AACA magazine, with an application blank to send back to us. People spend the $9. to express mail vendor applications back, because it's done on a first-come basis. People will even come right to the door of the Hershey Region office and be there when we come in.

The car show is run rather differently. AACA members enter their car in the show and pay a $15 entry fee. We give them a dash plaque that costs us $4 or so. We used to give each of them a present of some sort, a toy truck or umbrella or something, but it got too expensive. All of the car show money goes to AACA's national office.

Hershey Region makes its money from the flea market spaces. Each 10 x 30 foot space rents for $51 from Tuesday through Saturday, and there are 10,200 spaces. But that's still a good deal for the vendors, at about $10 a space per day. Whatever money we have left at the end of the year, we keep to get us started for the next year.

People can't believe that we do everything with volunteers. But there are many parts of the old car hobby. Being a vendor is one part of the hobby. Being a car show exhibitor is one part of the hobby. Being a car restorer is one part of the hobby. Being a judge at the car show is one part of the hobby. Putting on the Hershey meet is one part of the hobby. There are many ways to be involved with these old cars, different ways that can be enjoyable and interesting. You just have to do it.

—*Nelson Neff*
AACA Hershey Region Historian

they can use. But Hershey attracts large corporations, too. Companies that do most of their business with antique car enthusiasts have a large presence at Hershey. *Hemmings Motor News*, for example, has a tent in each swap meet field selling books and magazine subscriptions. Eastwood sells models and restoration supplies, Coker Tire offers reproduction tires in a bewildering variety of sizes, A&M Softseal has weatherstripping and other rubber parts, Classic Motorbooks puts up an enormous tent full of books on antique cars, motorcycles, airplanes and tractors.

As Motorbooks founder Tom Warth says, "I first came to Hershey in 1968

UNDER THE BENIGN gaze of the Milton Hershey School, late afternoon shoppers look for small parts. Notice the variety of carts used to haul treasures around.

THIS 1948 PACKARD station wagon is all there and very rare. It will make a superb prize for some lucky restorer. Unlike wood-bodied wagons from the twenties and thirties, these later woodies are mostly steel with only small wood inserts.

THE FUTURE HITS
Hershey; Amerivox
Prepaid Phone Cards are
just one of the many
unexpected services
available at Hershey,
from electric carts for
handicapped shoppers to
ATMs for instant cash.

THE FUTURE HITS
Hershey; Amerivox
Prepaid Phone Cards are
just one of the many
unexpected services
available at Hershey,
from electric carts for
handicapped shoppers to
ATMs for instant cash.

with a folding card table and an Econoline van full of books. As we grew, I'd
bring a dozen friends from Minneapolis, all volunteers, and we'd drive straight
through to save on expenses and stay in some fleabag motel out on the Harrisburg Turnpike. It was all great fun. Anyone who's anyone in the old car hobby
is at Hershey and we'd always run into them sooner or later."

And that, of course, is why everyone else is here, because everyone else is
here! Hobbyists or businessmen, neophytes or old-timers, everyone ends up at
Hershey. If you've never joined the throng, you've missed the most pleasantly-
exciting weekend of the old car hobby. You wouldn't think so, perhaps, but just
being on the field with all those other collectors and their cars and parts is a
terrific adrenalin high. People get red-in-the-face, out-of-breath excited at Hershey,
the way they do at a closely fought World Series game or a NASCAR race that
comes down to the last lap. Hershey is genuinely exciting, even if you don't
buy a darn thing all weekend. Just being part of it is enough.

SURROUNDED BY parts, this overall-clad shopper looks rather pensive.

Automobilia

Enthusiasts are hoarding all sorts of collectibles, some directly related to cars and some only distantly connected

A MASSACHUSETTS bike shop brought a Ryder truck full of antique two-wheelers to Hershey, priced from under $100 to over $2000. At that, these prices are at the bottom of the market for the respective models.

to four-wheel transportation. Such things as classic bicycles, motorcycles, promotional models, spin-dizzy racers, petroliana, paintings, sculpture, license plates, tag toppers, old trophies...anything is collectible these days.

Collecting these auto-related items is big business, about $700-million in annual sales, according to Eric Killorin of *Mobilia* magazine. At Hershey, you'll see everything from $20,000 Lalique radiator mascots to $200 tin toys to rows of people selling Hot Wheels toys from the seventies, still in blister packs, for $4.95. Literally anything is a collectible to somebody.

TANK-STYLE BIKES from the fifties are especially popular with Baby Boomers who remember pedaling them when new.

(FRONT TO REAR)
1936 VL 80 cubic inch
Harley-Davidson, made
to race on flat tracks;
original factory Harley
sidecar rig called a
Topper; 1946 Indian
Chief; 1955 Harley
panhead V-twin in an '85
softail frame; 1947 EL
knucklehead; 1946 UL
flathead. The cheapest
bike in the row is priced
at $7500; the restored EL
and UL are in the
$40,000 range!

MOTORCYCLES

Ford Model As and flathead V-8s may be the heart of the hobby, but interest has broadened to include all sorts of old machines, most of which you couldn't have given away a few years ago. Take old motorcycles, for example, one of the hottest collector markets right now. Motorcycles tend to be rarer than old cars of the same age, easier to restore, easier to garage and just as evocative of a particular time and place.

Four groups of motorcycles are especially prized. Almost any Harley-Davidson or Indian is collectible, with rare prewar models bringing up to $50,000. Factory-built racing machines, like the famous Norton Manx, Ducati Gran Sport or Matchless G50 have sold at auction for over $100,000. High-performance Italian street machines—the two-wheel equivalent of a Ferrari—like the Ducati Super Sport or MV Agusta Sport are bringing $25,000. Mid-sixties "cafe racers," especially Triumph or Vincent-powered Nortons, are also extremely collectible. As with cars, rarity and condition are all-important.

MOTORBIKES AND SCOOTERS

Prices range from about $150 to $10,000 for collector bikes, depending on rarity. Most popular are the famous Whizzer motorbikes from the late-forties/early-fifties, probably because so many middle-age men cut their motoring teeth—and knuckles—trying to get their Whizzers to run. Concours-quality Whizzers are selling in the $4,500 range, there's an active support group and even an AACA judging class. A restored Whizzer is probably the least expensive means to earn an AACA Senior First.

Motorscooters have taken off, too. Crude Cushmans, quirky Allstates, stylish Vespas and sophisticated Lambrettas are all being collected, restored and shown. Compared to a Whizzer, a scooter is a more difficult restoration—like a car, it has bodywork—but compared to a car or motorcycle, a scooter is as simple as dirt. Prices range from almost nothing to $10,000 for truly rare and significant Harley Toppers or Cushman Eagles. A factory sidecar adds even more value. Off-beat brands like the Skat-Kitty or Rupp have their own followings. Like any other collector item, the big things to look for are authenticity, eye appeal and condition, condition, condition.

(LEFT) AN ENVIABLE line-up of motorbikes ready for judging in AACA Class 5D. Whizzer and Sportsman models form the bulk of motorbike concours. (Below) A pristine Whizzer for sale at $4,500, the going rate for a fully-restored bike in #1 condition.

Place Your Order for

AGRICO

AVIATIO
(SUMMER)

PROBABLY THE MOST
valuable things are the
used oil cans and old
filling station signs,
what's now called
"petroliana." Those early
glass oil bottles are
especially neat in their
original racks, and now
sell for $50 each.

A VAST SELECTION OF neat petroliana, including a rare Gulfpride oil can rack from the fifties and a Sunoco sign from the thirties.

Petroliana

Aside from car models, the most popular segment of automobilia is memorabilia from gas stations and petroleum companies. "Petroliana," we call it. Petroliana ranges from service station "rest room" signs you dig out of the trash to antique gas pumps that are bringing $25,000 apiece. At Hershey, you can discover items from both ends of the petroliana spectrum, and most price points in between.

The best petroliana has a feeling of great nostalgia and charm, a feeling of going back in time, an evocative aura that's often more potent than the nostalgia of old cars themselves. Few people have personal associations with Duesenbergs, for example, but most of us recall the heft of a Mobil oil can with Pegasus on the side.

Petroliana is a way of owning not merely a car from the past, but of creating a whole automotive environment that dates to a specific period in time. Petroliana is such a wide subject that it leaves open the possibility of collecting almost anything automotive. A fellow named Jeff Pedersen has one of the largest petroliana collections in the United States, with over 18,000 separate items in his private museum, What's he got? Anything and everything that you can imagine that relates to the retail petroleum industry from oil cans and oil can racks to gas pumps and neon signs.

Petroliana collecting started with gasoline pumps, worth literally nothing twenty years ago. Today, rare originals are bought and sold for well over $20,000. As with old cars or almost any other antique, condition and originality are all-important. The very first gas pumps appeared in 1885, even before the automobile, handling kerosene and white gas. Most were built by Sylvanus Bowser in Fort Wayne, Indiana. By 1906, the first of rival John Tokheim's hand-powered gas pumps were on the street. Tokheim eventually became the standard service station gasoline pump, and the Tokheim Oil Tank and Pump Company the General Motors of gasoline pumps. Among the most collectible items of petroliana is Tokheim's Cut Number 850 Volumeter pump from the early-thirties. This is the classic cylindrical pump, decorated by a round dial with hands like a clock face and a lighted glass globe. Good ones have steadily increased in value even as old car prices fell in the late-eighties.

Gas pumps are simple devices compared to an automobile, but you'd be surprised at the hours you can spend restoring one that might be, when it's completed, worth less than a mint original. On the other hand, most gas pumps lived out in the weather, so mint originals are rare and consequently very pricey.

Gas pump globes form a whole separate area of petroliana, unique unto

AS COLLECTIBLE AS one can get, this Tokheim Cut Number 850 was a popular gas pump around 1932. Examples in this condition, original or restored, are very rare.

ORIGINAL GAS CANS, including one with the Mobil gargoyle, would be more collectible in less rusty condition, but are still desirable and very beautiful as art objects.

TOKHEIM PUMPS FROM
the early-fifties combine
streamlined styling and
numeric computers with
old-fashioned glass
advertising globes.

themselves. You can see literally hundreds, maybe thousands of these attractive glass advertising signs at Hershey. Prices range from under $100 to over $3,500, depending on age, condition and oil company insignia. Once again, condition, originality and rarity determine the prices. You might have to spend $2,000 for a globe made for the Sioux Oil Company in Wyoming during the thirties; a very late 13.5-inch Exxon globe from 1980 might be overpriced at $100.

As with any other area in the old car hobby—any other area of art or antiques—petroliana is rife with fakes and copies, not to mention poor restorations that have ruined the value of the original piece. Reproduction gas pump globes are a fact of life. As long as they're sold as repros, at a repro price, no problem. But can you tell a new reproduction globe from a mint original? You'd better be able to distinguish one from the other before you head for Hershey, cash in hand.

Early gas pump globes were made of one piece of glass, with the name of the fuel company usually etched or baked on. Their heyday was from around

1910 to 1930, and they are by far the most popular and consequently most expensive gas globes, with prices that start around $500 and go up into the thousands. A simpler type of globe has a drum made of plastic, metal or glass, with glass inserts on either end to carry the all-important logo. These three-piece globes were easier to make and repair, and consequently are now considered less collectible. They stayed in production right up into the sixties. Prices range from under $100 to nearly $1,000.

THIS TEXACO TIN SIGN from the mid-thirties still mentions the Texas Company, dropped from Texaco signage after a redesign by industrial designer Walter Dorwin Teague in 1937.

Collectors started buying up old globes in the late sixties, and by 1975 or so, there were already companies making reproduction globes. There's nothing wrong with a reproduction as long as it is neither bought nor sold as genuine.

How do you tell the difference? Most noticeably by the modern paint used to create the logo on the inside of the globe. It is possible to have such paint chemically analyzed, but realistically, comparison of a new, bright shiny globe with an original globe shows the difference. Some reproduction globes are dated in the base. In the old days, three-piece globes with metal frames were all 15 inches or 16.5 inches in diameter. Many reproduction metal-framed globes are only 13.5 inches in diameter. This makes them very easy to spot, once you know. Of course, original 13.5 inch glass faces may have been put into a reproduction frame, which makes things more confusing. As with most other collectibles, the basic rule of thumb is if a deal seems too good to be true, it probably is.

Enamelled metal signs are another area to be careful about. Companies like Eastwood or Griot's Garage sell a wide range of new metal signs at very reasonable prices. You wouldn't want to buy one at a swap meet thinking it's an original. Period signs tend to be more visually arresting. In the old days, gas stations were identified by signs carrying the oil company logo. Most of these signs were stamped steel and painted with porcelainized enamel like an early exhaust header or a bathtub. Such signs—particularly if equipped with neon lights—can carry five-figure pricetags today.

The Holy Grail, of course, is to find a complete service station, preferably one of those very stylized architectural gems from the twenties, thirties or forties. Standardized stations were designed for each major oil company, as alike as McDonald's restaurants, some by architects whose names are still well known. Architects like Walter Dorwin Teague, Frederick G. Frost and Herbert O. Alden created memorable standardized station designs. Petroliana buffs try to buy or replicate such stations, then recreate the atmosphere of a specific place in time.

This is not as far-fetched as it sounds. In every small town in America there is at least one filling station that hasn't been changed in any substantial way since it was built decades ago. Often, a residential neighborhood has grown up around such a landmark, and zoning prohibits operating it as a commercial gas station. Such important examples of petroliana can often be snapped up for peanuts. The downside, of course, is that there may be underground gas tanks that will get you in trouble with the EPA. If you do get interested in buying your own station to house your petroliana collection, be careful.

Once you have your own station, everything becomes fair game. You can head for Hershey and buy period gas cans, oil cans, oil can racks, parts in NOS

PETROLIANA OF Sinclair High-Compression Gasoline is among the most sought after, therefore some of the most expensive. In various guises, Sinclair has been selling gasoline since Harry Sinclair started the company in 1916. Even a heavily damaged sign like this has great value because of its size and originality.

IT CAN BE HARD TO
tell the difference
between reproduction
and original signs and
globes like these.

boxes, signage, an oil company clock, a period Coke machine, a phone booth with a phone from the appropriate era, posters, calendars, magazines, oil company maps, gas coupons from World War II, hats, uniforms and coveralls, an old-fashioned center-post lift, period jacks and tools, promotional models, old *Motor* manuals. The possibilities for petroliana are absolutely endless.

There are people doing this right now, people with full-blown service stations filled with petroliana. But there's always somebody willing to take any good idea one step further. From Bill Taormina's Billy's Service Station in Anaheim, California, to Terry Ehrich's Hemmings Sunoco in Bennington, Vermont, there are petroliana collectors across the country who've trumped the more timid players and actually opened for business in old-time service stations, dispensing gas with a smile, checking oil and washing windshields without being asked. At Billy's, the attendants even wear those peaked caps and short-sleeve white shirts with a black bow tie that formed the uniform of servitude for generations of gas pump jockeys. Petroliana can mean anything you want it to be.

LICENSE PLATES

The first automobilia collectors concentrated on license plates—often nailing them to the garage walls—and plates are still very popular. Most valuable are the early porcelainized number plates with raised state insignia that were used at the very dawn of motoring. Matched pairs of these early plates can cost $2,000 or more. On the other hand, a single number plate stamped out of aluminum by the millions is worth no more than a few dollars. There are old car collectors who buy period plates from the same year their car was built, but diehard number plate collectors wouldn't dream of soiling their valuable collectibles by actually mounting them on a car, and down near the dirty road, besides. Glass cases and camel hair brushes only, for them.

AN ASSORTMENT OF plates decorates a Hershey booth. Prices range from $3 to in the hundreds, depending on year and state. As a general rule, older plates from states with fewer cars are worth more.

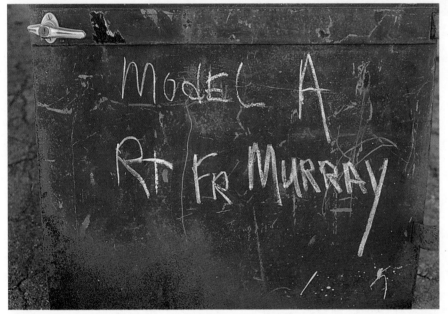

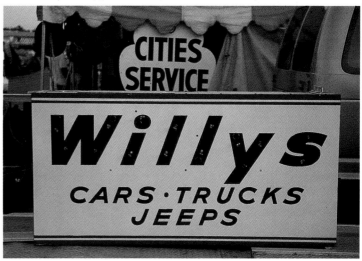

WHAT COULD BE MORE winsome than this mid-thirties pedal car, vaguely reminiscent of a '37 Ford? Restored, it's worth as much or more than the real car.

THIS STEELCRAFT
Steam-roller, made in Murray, Ohio, is a rare tin toy. It's big enough for a toddler to sit on the roof, push with his feet and steer with the wheel disguised as the top of the smokestack.

TOY CARS

The heart of the automobilia market is what collectors call "miniatures on four wheels" and what you and I call toy cars. This mostly consists of new models. People snap up the surprisingly precise Italian Burago models you buy for $29.95 at places like K-Mart. They grab oil company truck and airplane models at the local filling station for $19.95. The Franklin Mint and Danbury Mint sell $100-million worth each year of high-end 1/43rd models priced anywhere from $129 to $500 each. Then there are hundreds of model builders producing custom-made models that cost from $5,000 to $50,000 depending on their intricacy, percentage of "scratchbuilt" parts, scale and quality.

THE PEDAL CAR
styled like a '56 Pontiac convertible, the Red Crown gasoline sign that once decorated the front of a filling station and the Studebaker dealer sign are especially neat.

All these models are new, but they're very collectible because of their craftsmanship and high level of detail. These models are marketed and promoted as collectibles, and people buy them as collectibles. Only time will tell if they're truly going to appreciate in value as their buyers hope.

Just as car people buy the cars that they couldn't afford when they were teenagers, toy car collectors collect the things that interested them when they were children. One result is that just as interest in Brass Era cars has dwindled along with men who remember them new, interest in pressed-steel toys and pedal cars is dwindling along with the number of people who can remember playing with them as children. This doesn't mean that metal toy trucks and cars made by Kingsbury, Buddy L, Structo, Keystone and similar companies are no longer valuable. They can sell for many thousands of dollars. Original, little-used pedal cars made by a manufacturer like Gendron during the thirties or forties are even pricier. Some of these pedal cars have topped $40,000, more than the full-size cars they mimic! But long-term, interest in pedal cars will cool, as the collectors who remember them die off.

What will replace them as the hot collectibles? Toy cars and models that Baby Boomers played with as young children are the current place to invest your money. These 35- to 50-year-olds probably didn't have a pedal car as a kid, pedal cars were already *passé* by then. Instead, the children of the late-fifties to early-seventies were raised on slot cars and plastic model kits. Hess Oil toy tank trucks, Tonka toy trucks and similar steel toys are surprisingly valuable, but they are not where the action is.

Monogram and Revell plastic models—the ones you could buy for $1.98 in the sixties—are now selling for hundreds of dollars. That's for unbuilt models still in the original box. One collector I know bought hundreds of these models over the years, stacking them in his basement, still in the boxes. He expects

MOBILIA

My idea for *Mobilia* magazine started when I went to Hershey in 1991. I was blown away by the amount of non-car stuff there was for sale on the field. There were model kits and signage and all these other items in between the '57 Chevy hubcaps and the Model T windshield wiper motors.

A lot of the stuff seemed to be things I remembered from the sixties, Monogram model kits I'd built as a kid and things like that. These were being sold for $100, as collectibles. So I bought a few things, and like any fanatical hobbyist, I started looking for information on automobilia.

The only thing I could find was the automobilia section of *Hemmings Motor News*. I talked to my friend Dave Brownell, from *Hemmings*, and he wasn't very encouraging. He said, "Oh, there's only a few hundred people interested in this stuff."

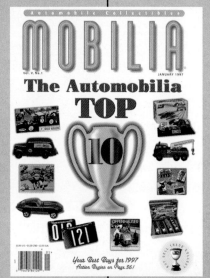

I saw a whole group of people collecting automobilia. It was a very fragmented group, extending into antique cars, and toys and traditional antiques. But it was also a large group of people. I bought some mailing lists and started a magazine. And now, just a few years later, we have 26,000 subscribers and a going business that started because of the Hershey swap meet.

Hershey played a pivotal role in my life. It seemed like every other vendor space I saw in 1991 had model kits, toy trucks, pedal cars, gas pumps, old picnic sets. Everything and anything. License plates, of course. And Hershey is so huge. I figured if all these people were here with this stuff, there had to be a market for a publication. And there was.

—*Eric Killorin*
Publisher, Mobilia

to retire on what they'll be worth in a couple of decades, and no doubt he's right. The value of these models has skyrocketed. Plastic models stuck together by a nine-year-old have almost no value to a collector, though the same model, built today by an adult professional modeler, can soar into the thousands if the detail and accuracy are elaborate enough.

The appeal of models? Collectors can have a whole collection in a closet, a collection that cost peanuts. As Eric Killorin says, "They're spouse-proof." If you come home with a Ferrari, you're in trouble. A model Ferrari? No problem.

In another whole category are promotional models and stylists' scale models. Promos were given out or sold by car dealers, particularly in the forties and fifties, as a way to promote new car sales. Prices range from $100 or so into the thousands for rare examples.

Stylists' models are much rarer. These large scale models were used to show styling concepts to either the individual clients of an independent coachbuilder or the management of a car manufacturer. The best of these models sell for $10,000 or more. Pricier still are stylists' models for cars that were never built.

ANTIQUE PEDAL CARS have grown into a major area of collector interest, particularly if they're as recognizable as the '53 Chevy on the left or the '58 Plymouth on the right. Pedal cars in this condition will probably get restored to match some owner's example of the real thing. Even $200 is too much to pay for this Plymouth, but it will sell for over $2,000 when restored. That's still half as much as an unrestored mint original.

TOY TRUCKS AND HEAVY equipment are immensely popular and consequently expensive. Why? A whole car collection fits on your desktop.

A '59 PLYMOUTH
flanks a '64 Rambler 440.
In minature, of course.
The John Deere tractor
pedal car will be very
collectible in the future.

At Hershey last year, for example, well-known collectibles dealer Charlie Schalebaum was offering a model of a four-passenger Corvette created by GM Styling. Asking price; $45,000.

Automobilia can be almost anything. *Hemmings Motor News* editor Dave Brownell is a major collector of Brass Era headlamps, which he rightly considers limited-edition sculpture. Interestingly enough, while the market for Brass Era cars is quite soft, prices for brass headlamps are rising steadily. Like thousands of other collectors, Brownell has a house full of such stuff. He's not alone. Indeed, his purchases seem relatively mainstream.

Vintage racer and Hershey stalwart Joel Finn owns dozens of cars and a whole archive full of photos and literature. But he also has such unusual bits of automobilia as the shift lever from Juan Manuel Fangio's 250F Maserati and a connecting rod from Jules Goux's Peugeot that won the Indy 500 in 1913. I myself own such oddities as the fiberglass bucket seat from Jimmy Clark's World Championship Lotus 25, Craig Vetter's original styling model for a full-bodied motorcycle that broke a world record for minimal fuel consumption and the four-carb intake manifold off the Allard raced by SAC General Curtis LeMay in the early-fifties.

Anything automotive, and I do mean *anything*, is being collected by somebody as automobilia. I know a guy who prizes Carroll Shelby's pillowcase, another who treasures a bit of the wreckage from James Dean's Porsche. Are these the modern equivalents of pieces of the True Cross? Not really. It's more like the glass case of novelties that adorned Victorian parlors; an ostrich egg, an eagle feather, a meteorite, an ashtray from the Philadelphia Exposition and an autograph of Lord Baden-Powell. Harmless trinkets with value only to their owners and amateur enthusiasts similarly afflicted.

A MIXED BAG OF RARE stuff including promotional tire manufacturer ashtrays, a streamlined Texaco gas truck, a ceramic Indy car decanter and an early-thirties Buddy L truck with unique Pull-N-Ride handle. Large-scale Buddy L toys like this are priced from $600 up.

HOOD ORNAMENTS were one of the great art forms of the twenties and thirties. In their day, Packard's "goddess of speed" or Lincoln's grayhound were as well-known as Nike's "swoosh" is today. About the only hood ornaments that still retain their panache are the leaping cat of Jaguar, the three-pointed star or Mercedes-Benz and the "flying lady" of Rolls-Royce. (Clockwise from top left) A Buick goddess, the hand-made gunsight of the 1919 Shaw Special Indy racer, a famous Packard pelican (which Packard collectors prefer to call a cormorant), a winged airfoil from an air-cooled Franklin, a Lincoln grayhound, and a lighted crystal Lalique indian mounted on a Packard hood. The winged goddess on the opposite page decorates a Cadillac.

AUTOMOTIVE ART

Each year, usually on Thursday evening, there's an automotive art and literature auction at the Hotel Hershey. Typically, there will be 500 different objects for sale, often previously owned by famous collectors like Henry Austin Clark, Peter Helck, Briggs Cunningham or Alec Ulmann. Some are inexpensive, in the $100 range, but some, like a Montaut poster for Pneu Michelin, are expected to sell for $7,000-$8,000. Oil paintings of automotive subjects, say a large Peter Helck, are in the $100,000 league these days.

Who buys automotive art? A vast array of collectors, most of whom also have garages full of cars. Who sells automotive art? Everyone from Charlie Schalebaum to Christie's auction house. Popular items include hand-colored Brass Era lithographs by Montaut and Gamy, evocative charcoal drawings from the thirties by Geo Ham, Impressionist racing watercolors from the fifties by Walter Gotschke, and modern works by Ken Dallison and Peter Helck.

A group of artists called the Automotive Fine Arts Society has tried to raise the prices of contemporary paintings and sculpture, and has been, to a certain degree, successful. But the free market will ultimately determine values, which may be based on very different criteria than professional artists would use to judge a work of art.

A perfect case in point is sculptor Stanley Wanlass, whose bronze sculptures were very popular for a few years. As Charlie Schalebaum was quoted recently in *AutoWeek* as saying, "Wanlass sculptures used to double in value after a few years; now they're worth half their original price." Mr. Wanlass can take solace in the fact that depreciation is common in contemporary art...just before a period of rapid appreciation starts.

THE GEORGE VANDERBILT Cup carries the names of the winners of the 1936 and '37 Vanderbilt Cup races held at Roosevelt Field, on Long Island. Tazio Nuvolari won in 1936 with his Alfa Romeo Grand Prix car; Bernd Rosemeyer won in 1937 in an Auto Union.

Camp Hershey

It's a city of thousands that appears overnight in a Pennsylvania field, stays for five days, then disappears

THIS STAINLESS STEEL over-the-road GMC bus from the early-fifties is not only a valuable collectors item—prices start around $10,000 and go up sharply—but also makes a motorhome with oodles of panache.

for another twelve months. Housing runs the gamut from college kids who stretch out on the seats of their old Chevy and nap for a few hours to wealthy collectors safely ensconced in motorhomes that cost more than most people's houses and have nicer accommodations. The average swap meet visitor travels somewhere in the mid-range, with a modest motorhome, camping trailer or conversion van packed with friends or family, food and drink and stuff to sell in the swap meet. Or stuff they just bought in the swap meet. Or both.

A common interest in old cars builds friendships

SPICED ONLY BY THE
pungent smell of lighter
fluid and barbecue ribs,
Pennsylvania dusk settles
over the peaceful camp of
the Hershey army.

instantly at Hershey. Many campers arrange to meet friends from previous years and camp together, or they meet on the way and caravan to Hershey, chattering about old cars on their CBs as they roll along, full of high expectations.

Vendors can camp right at their swap meet space. Shoppers congregate in camping areas rented out by Herco, the holding company that controls most of Hershey's service businesses. For a nominal fee, Herco provides septic pickup and disposal. Showers are even available at the Herco maintenance building. Other campers prefer Hershey's High Meadow Campgrounds on the banks of Swatara Creek, complete with two swimming pools, country store, laundry, cable TV hookup and regular shuttle buses to the swap meet.

As you might expect, every hotel, motel and B&B for a radius of 50 miles is booked solid on Hershey weekend. Many swap meet shoppers stay half an hour away in York, Harrisburg, Lancaster or even Reading. Amazingly enough,

MODEST CAMPERS LIKE these are the norm at Hershey, just right for being in the middle of all the action. These families are actually parked in the driveway to HersheyPark.

traffic is not a problem. Thanks to eager beaver shoppers who are on their way to the swap meet before dawn and late-rising spectators who are in no particular rush, traffic spreads out over the morning. Realistically, there's no reason not to stay in York or Lancaster.

Except, well, you won't be at the center of the action. To really do Hershey in the proper style, you need either an antique truck camper—maybe a reproduction of the Ford AA campers that Henry Ford and Thomas Edison used for roughing it in the twenties or a Pierce Arrow trailer from the thirties—a period camper or trailer from the sixties, or best of all, an old bus ingeniously converted to a roomy motorhome. The classics among motorhomes are the front-wheel drive GMCs from the Seventies, conversions of stainless steel long-haul buses from the early-fifties or conversions of the rounded schoolbuses built by Crown to California state specifications and unchanged for decades.

Among old car buffs, the unique, the unusual, the *unexpected* carries the highest status. Anybody can go to his local RV center and write a check; not everybody can restore an old Greyhound bus then tastefully redo the interior like a Concordia yawl. Craftsmanship, artistry, attention to detail and creativity are more highly prized than mere dollars. The secret competition at Hershey is not among the swap meet vendors, the car show exhibitors or the car corral salesmen. It takes place in the evenings, when the campers examine each others rigs. It's not AACA-sanctioned, but it's very real, nonetheless.

Hershey Mud

THIS GUY HAS THE right idea in Hershey fashions—Hawaiian shirt, jeans and boots. Now all he needs is Mud+Snow tires for his shopping cart.

Read General Robert E. Lee's letters home, and you'll find a lot of comment about the mud of Central Pennsylvania. Indeed, in some ways the spring and fall mud seasons determined the course of the Civil War. The mud made the roads impassable back then, just as it makes the Hershey swap meet rows impassable today. There is no solution. Put an army of 250,000 people in a farmer's field, have it rain for a day or so—which it always seems to do in early October—and the field is going to turn to mud. No surprise there. The only thing to do is wear a smile. And your Wellies.

Chocolate-colored, chocolate-textured—but not as tasty—Hershey's mud is as famous as its chocolate, at least among old car buffs. "How was the mud this year?" ask those who had to stay at home. And they expect to hear about every squishy step. "Was it as bad as '94? As bad as '75? Remember when that guy lost his boots!" We all evaluate the Hershey experience the way the editors at *Wine Connoisseur* rank cabernet sauvignon. "1977? A great year. Lots of sun, long evenings. Found some fuel-pump parts. Didn't need my boots once."

PHOTOGRAPHER JEAN Constantine crosses rain-created "Lake Hershey" in the Chocolate Field. Her cameras are tucked safely under her pink poncho.

YEP, LOOKS LIKE MEADE'S army went through here this morning. We'll probably catch up with 'em around Gettysburg.

A TYPICAL HERSHEY
landscape: tents, trailers, motorhomes, shoppers, standing water and mud

Buy. Sell. Trade. Collect.

Hershey's car corral is sensory overload for a car nut. Every old car, and there are 1,800 in this one parking lot, holds some different memory, some different promise. If you could only own them all. There are guys who try.

THE DASHBOARD OF A very rare 1906 Stanley Gentleman's Speedy Roadster. Not exactly the kind of car you expect to see for sale in a swap meet, even at Hershey. The wonderful brass instruments measure steam pressure.

We met a collector and his friend in the campground. They had come all the way from Florida to sell a '55 Thunderbird they'd picked up at Hershey the year before. And they did. They sold it for more than they expected.

So now they had $30,000 burning holes in their pockets. They found a '56 Lincoln convertible, a '40 Ford and a Cadillac Seville they could afford if they threw in a few thousand more. Then they had to buy a second trailer to get everything home. Their plan was to finish restoring the Lincoln and the Ford—both were almost done—and bring them back next year.

AN IDENTICAL STANLEY Gentleman's Speedy Roadster recorded 84.7 mph at Ormond Beach in 1906. The primitive non-condensing steam engine connects directly to the rear wheels and produces about 50 hp. The gas-fired boiler lives under the hood. Range? About 60 miles before you have to stop for water.

A RUBBER BELT DRIVE and centrifugal clutch tell us this isn't a real 1903 Curved Dash Oldsmobile. Looks like just the thing for shopping at Sun City Leisure World, though.

Imagine when these guys gets home. Instead of emptying one bay of the garage, they've added two more cars to the total.

The car corral reflects the state of the old car hobby. Prices of Brass Era cars are very weak, particularly those of Model T Fords which can be snapped up for almost nothing. Less desirable body styles like two-door and four-door sedans or older restorations bring under $5,000.

Inexpensive special-interest cars from the twenties and thirties are so out of favor you hardly even see any in the car corral. Major classics from the twenties and thirties now show up in the car corral, something that didn't happen a few years ago when expensive cars like this were offered only through fancy auctions. As prices for major classics have dropped, their owners have obviously decided to show them to the Hershey crowds. You never know where a buyer is lurking.

The hottest segments of the market are now postwar American performance cars, racing cars, sports cars, hot rods and European exotics. You'll see all of them in the Hershey car corral. There has been a lot of publicity in the general interest press about the precipitous fall in prices of exotic sports cars, particularly Ferrari and Jaguar models. What didn't get reported is that the prices of many less expensive sports cars have actually risen since the peak of the old car boom in 1988 and '89. MGAs, Triumph TR-3s and similar small British two-seaters have crossed the $25,000 barrier. That's a new phenomenon.

Another is the boom in hot rods. I know men who have spent in excess of $300,000 to restore an old hot rod. What are they thinking of? Opinions have changed. Hot rods used to be considered despicable destruction of original old

THIS 1933 AMERICAN Austin is actually a British Austin Seven made under license by the American Austin Company. These tiny 750cc, 13 hp minicars were produced for two decades after their debut in 1922, while the engine continued in production until 1962. Thanks to licensing agreements, Sevens were built by many different companies, including BMW in Germany, Rosengart in France and Datsun in Japan.

BY FAR THE HARDEST type of car to sell is one like this '39 Buick sedan that's been "personalized" by its New Jersey artist/owner. The chances of finding another person with exactly your taste is slim, while the car probably isn't valuable enough to bother trying to return it to stock condition.

HERSHEY'S CAR CORRAL is the largest antique car sales area in the world, with over 1,300 spaces. The cars in the immediate foreground of this photo give a hint of the kinds of vehicles available, including a rare 1930 Cadillac phaeton, an even rarer 1941 Packard One Twenty four-door convertible, a Bricklin, a '58 Buick and a Ford AA truck carrying a fairgrounds carousel.

cars; now at least some collectors and dealers—Kirk F. White, for one—have realized that the best hot rods were built with enviable craftsmanship by men whose names are now legendary. So hot rod prices have zoomed through the roof, fueled by an appreciation for this handmade artistry.

Real estate brokers stress "location, location, location." According to Steve Ferguson, editor of the *N.A.D.A. Collectible Car Appraisal Guide*, the equivalent for old car buyers should be "condition, condition, condition." As Steve puts it, "When valuing exotic and collectible cars, the overall condition, mileage and originality of the vehicle are major factors."

How do you measure these things? Well, you have to know what you're doing, or if you don't know, you have to find someone who does. This is not rocket science. You evaluate an antique or collectible car the same way you'd evaluate a normal used car. The superficial condition should be fairly obvious. You don't need a mechanic to tell a good paint job from a bad one, a ripped interior from a perfect one, a dirty engine compartment from a clean one.

Where it gets tricky is knowing what's underneath the surface glitter. Bad bodywork, or good bodywork over a bad structure, is sometimes difficult even for an expert to spot. Unfortunately, heavy structural work is by far the most expensive part of any restoration. Welding new unibody panels requires time and skill, which means money. By comparison, rebuilding an engine or replacing the transmission is child's play.

THE DEALER

I've got five vehicles here and my friend has five vehicles, everything from a Rolls-Royce to a Trabant. This Mack truck wouldn't be considered even very big at the truck shows we go to. I used it to pull a trailer with my cars on it, and I decided that since it's here, I might as well offer it for sale. I won't need it until Hershey again next year, and by then I can find another one. I got this one in a swap with a friend. It only has 38,000 miles on it.

Hershey is the only show we come to. We're only from Allentown, but it's still a lot of preparation to bring 10 cars out here. This is our business. Hershey is a lark for some people, but it's bread and butter for me. It's getting crazy. I used to be able to sell 60 percent

of the cars I brought to Hershey. Now there are 1,700 cars in the car corral, plus there are a lot more out there in the flea market.

That makes it tough to compete. There are a few impulse buyers, but most people come to Hershey because they want a particular type of car.

We bring our motorhome down here 10 days ahead, so we can get the parking spot we want. Then we have to pay for 10 days of parking. We used to show up at 4 A.M. on Tuesday to get the car corral spot we wanted, but now you can register ahead for a specific spot. So that makes it easier. But this weekend is still a lot of work.
—*Tom Troxell*
Car Corral Vendor

PROBABLY THE CUTEST car Ford ever made, the 1939 Deluxe Convertible was also the last Ford built with a rumble seat in the trunk. Thanks to 85 hp from its famous flathead V-8, this was considered a high-performance car in its day with a top speed around 90 MPH, 0 to 60 in just over 20 seconds.

Many enthusiasts figure they can have a car painted for next to nothing, so they'll buy an otherwise solid old car and think they've picked up a bargain. In the old days, maybe. But not anymore. Thanks to environmental protection laws, modern bodyshops are almost required to have $100,000 spray booths, modern paint alone can easily cost over $1,000 for enough to paint a whole car, top-notch painters get $25 an hour these days and what with one thing and another, most bodyshops figure $2,000 for every week they put into your car, not including parts and supplies. Bottom line, this means the cheapest quality paint job is going to cost you $4,000, while cars being prepared for concours competition can easily have paint and bodywork bills that exceed $100,000. All of this is by way of explaining why condition is so important.

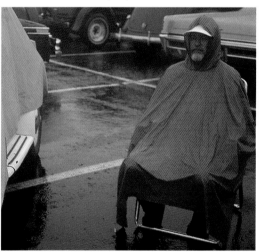

Another thing you should know is that it's almost impossible to get your money out of a professional restoration these days. Within reason, it costs little more to restore an expensive car than a cheap car. Which means that restoring the cheap car just does not make economic sense. I have a friend who spent $110,000 to restore a 1967 Camaro convertible to concours standards, then sold it at the top of the market for $25,000. This is not good business.

IT ALWAYS RAINS AT Hershey, even during the car corral. Smart sellers come prepared.

Originality is another critical factor. What do we mean by originality? Original means precisely what the car came with when it left the factory. To take a blatant example, let's say you're having trouble with the 6 volt electrical system on your 1937 Ford V-8. A helpful mechanic suggests switching over to a 12

**FABULOUS 1930
Packard Sport Phaeton
cost $4885 when new,
boasted 106 HP from
384.8 cubic inch I-8. This
one looks to be in
concours condition, but
getting that new top wet
could stain it and ruin the
car for AACA judging.**

volt system, which is all well and good. In the Speedway Motors catalog you come across a special mount to adapt a late-model General Motors alternator to your 60-year-old Ford engine. This will solve all your problems. But it will also take hundreds of dollars off the value of your car, because it's no longer the way Henry originally built it.

In this particular example, no problem. If you don't care about winning concours, you can drive your Ford with the reliable GM alternator and if anybody ever wants to switch back to a 1937 Ford generator, all it takes is a couple of bolts. The problem comes when you permanently alter a car by making an irreversible modification. Now you've truly destroyed the car's originality.

As an old car owner, you must be aware of such issues every time you work on your car. As a car corral shopper, you must know enough about this car to spot something that's not original. Anybody can tell the difference between a GM alternator and a Ford generator, but do you know the precise shade of Ford Brewster Green? A concours judge will deduct points for an non-original paint color, and there's no guarantee that just because a car is for sale in the Hershey car corral that it's original and proper. All too many people use the car corral as a way to dispose of cars that are otherwise unsaleable.

Let's say you've found the car of your dreams, that it is correct and original, that the price agrees with the prices of similar cars in *Hemmings Motor News* or the *N.A.D.A. Guide*. Now what? Well, you'd best have cash, because the car corral is "cash only." So you stop by the ATM, hand over the cash and get both a bill of sale and a transfer of title. The seller removes his license plates, shakes your hand and walks away. It's up to you to get this car out of Hershey's parking lot by Sunday morning. This means you better have come to Hershey with dealer plates, a trailer or the

phone number of somebody like Bob Pass at Passport Transport, who'll send a truck out to bring your prize home.

Every old car has something wrong with it. Now, you've just bought an antique car from somebody you just met, and you have no idea what may be wrong with it. Are you going to start driving to Sioux Falls, or are you going to put it on the trailer? I know what I'd do, but then I've been stranded by the side of the road a few too many times in newly purchased antiques. The rule of thumb

(ABOVE) HERSHEY IS tiring for this New Jersey artist.
(Below) Typical of the car corral, a whole row of '55, '56 and '57 Thunderbirds for sale.

THEY'RE ALL WOODIES!
'49 Dodge Coronet, '41
Plymouth Special Deluxe,
'48 Buick Roadmaster,
'47 Oldsmobile 66, '48
Chrysler Town & Country,
'35 Ford Station Wagon.

is to allow at least 10 percent of the price of any old car—20 percent is better—to make unforeseen repairs. This means, of course, that you must deduct this percentage from the price you're willing to pay for the car, or else be totally convinced that this one is something special, the one that won't need any repairs when you get it home. I've never come across a car like that yet.

Should you worry about the mileage that shows on the odometer? Not very much. An old car that's sat in a barn for forty years may show only a few thousand miles on the odometer, but may be a worthless piece of junk. Another car, with hundreds of thousands of miles, could be a much better buy if it's been conscientiously maintained. Condition and originality count for everything.

From one point of view, the car corral at Hershey is just a huge used car lot, not much different from Trusty Tom's Money Talks, Ain't Nobody Walks, out by the Dew Drop Inn. It's just that the cars are a lot older and a lot more expensive. And of course, Hershey has more cars on display than Trusty Tom. But the car corral is also a rolling history of the automobile; you can study anything from a 1903 Oldsmobile to a late-model Cadillac, including of course, cars you've never seen nor heard of before and probably won't see again unless they come back to Hershey next year.

The car corral is a powerful, poignant intersection of thousands of lives. There are people selling cars for any number of reasons, people buying cars for any number of reasons, people who wish they could sell cars, people who wish they could buy cars, people who just want to entertain their kids for the day, people who are trying to educate their kids in the fascination of these cool old machines so different from the modern cars they see every day.

The car corral is both a beginning and an ending, the place where one man's love affair with a particular automobile ends and another's begins. It is a place of giddy anticipation, of high hopes for both buyer and seller. The buyer is happy because he's just bought the car of his dreams. The seller is doubly happy, more often than not, both because he's sold this car and because he's already got his eye on the next one he wants to buy, restore and sell at Hershey next year.

In the end, though, the car corral is central to what the old car hobby is all about. Why do people chase after all that stuff in the swap meet? Mostly, they're looking for the parts they need to complete their latest project, the parts that will allow them to fulfill a promise made years or even decades before, a promise to breath new life into a derelict machine. Why do people show their completed cars in the concours? Because the concours reaffirms what they've accomplished, that they've rescued this car, that it has been brought back from the dead and that AACA experts recognize this rebirth.

LOOK AT THAT WOOD! A wooden car is more trouble than a wooden boat, particularly on a day as wet as this, but is so rich and warm and distinctive. No wonder we all have a special spot in our hearts for a woody.

US CORVETTE NUTS GO crazy for a line-up like this: '68 through '82 Corvettes like these are incredibly underpriced values in today's old car market.

The car corral is also about love, about commitment. There's a popular bumper sticker you'll see on the back of many racing cars that reads "She said it was either her or racing. And damn, I'm gonna miss her!" Just why no one has printed up a bunch that substitute "old cars" for "racing" I don't understand. The goal, after all, is preserving and driving these old cars, using them in the way they were intended to be used by their makers. And that takes a degree of dedication that is all too often lacking in our society. If nothing else, owning an old car teaches one commitment.

There are businessmen at Hershey, dispassionately evaluating just what they can sell that car for back home or what they can afford to sell it for, today, cash. But many more of the people you'll see cruising the car corral are dreamers, guys who lead with their heart, not their head, the ones who'll buy that old clunker and spend more than she'll ever be worth to restore her. You know what? These dreamers are the most important people at Hershey, because without them, none of this, not the swap meet, not the car show, not the car corral, would exist. The dreamers, and their willingness to invest make the hobby work.

I usually sleep in my van, shower at the Herco building, and then make lunch and dinner from snacks in the Society of Automotive Historians tent. I don't think you can do Hershey any cheaper.

— **ROBERT BELL**

Hospitality

Hershey is a five-day party. Different people party on different levels. You can stay in Lancaster or York, or the Hotel Hershey, and be as remote from the mud and dust of the swap meet as though you'd stayed on the moon. Or you can camp in the car and live on pizza and fried dough and have mud up to your knees. Or hit a happy medium.

SAVORING A QUIET moment, the chef from Hotel Hershey picks his own spices in the hotel's private herb garden.

Hershey's secret is that the town itself is already a tourist attraction, so the infrastructure for dealing with large groups of people is already in place—the restaurants, motels, parking lots and roads. The AACA adds another layer of convenience. For example, until it got out of hand, serious swap-meet shoppers would bring a golf cart or motorized bicycle for getting around the ever-expanding

AN AACA TRADITION.
Hershey volunteers sell
local apples and cider
along with programs in
the swap meet.

NO HEALTH FOOD HERE!
Long lines form for
sausage and french fries,
chili dogs and other
caloric fomentors of
agitazione. At least
they'll walk it off this
afternoon.

grounds. The organizers finally had to restrict such vehicles because they were
creating traffic jams of their own. The easy and practical solution was to provide
electric carts for handicapped or injured guests, which is what they've done.
Thousands of other details have to be covered too, like three ambulances and a
first aid center, telephones, souvenirs, and most importantly, food.

Hershey Region started a tradition decades ago of selling local apples and
apple cider from the program stands scattered throughout the grounds. This
tradition still continues. Herco controls all other food at Hershey, selecting sup-
pliers to sell a variety of foods at 50 separate locations. In four days, Hershey old
car buffs spend over $1-million on food at the concession stands, Herco keeps
no records, but we estimate the hordes consume 100,000 hot dogs, 75,000 ham-
burgers, 50,000 plates of french fries, 20,000 slices of pizza and 400,000 sodas.

America's eating habits have changed over the decades, and Hershey has
changed to reflect this. Nowadays, in addition to the traditional fast foods, you
can find vendors selling high-energy snacks like fruit, nuts, and of course, choco-

late in a wondrous variety of shapes and sizes.

Hershey's Chocolate World sells more gift items and serves more ice cream cones, milkshakes and chocolate bars during the swap meet than during any other week of the year.

Another Hershey tradition are the hospitality tents put up by many organizations and car clubs. Such unexpected groups as the Bugatti Owners Club and Rolls-Royce Owners Club offer their members and other interested enthusiasts a place to get dry, warm and, depending, less thirsty. Owl's Head Transportation Museum and similar automotive attractions have booths, while The Society of Automotive Historians goes all out to put on a regular buffet each evening.

Probably the most interesting social phenomenon at Hershey is the red ball concert. Organized by an informal group who raise a red balloon over their swap meet area in the evenings, this event brings together an ever-changing group of musicians who put on a free concert every night, just for fun. Traditions like this make Hershey so special.

THE TRUE NUTS AT Hershey are coated in Bavarian glaze. Could this be the origin of the Hershey Bar containing Almonds?

PIZZA AND A COKE ON a cold and rainy night in the swap meet. Makes you feel like the carnival has just left town.

World's Largest Car Show

Everyone always describes Hershey as "immense." With 35 miles of vendor aisles, the swap meet is immense, far larger than any other. With 1,300 old cars for sale, the car corral is immense, the largest antique car lot in the world. And with 2,000 entries, the car show is larger than any other antique car show.

THESE CHECKED COVERS on dual sidemount spares are intended to wow the judges into a higher score for this 1929 Marmon.

For many people, the highpoint of Hershey Week is the car show, more properly the AACA Eastern National Fall Meet. After a while they get tired of looking at antique parts and unabashed junk, and they're ready to see some *old cars.* And not just any old cars but the best AACA National level machines, as good as any in the world.

Many prestigious concours—Pebble Beach, Meadow Brook Hall, Amelia Island, Concours of the

THE HOT ONES—'55-'56-'57 Chevies—are among the most popular of all collector cars. And with good reason. They're handsome, nostalgic, well-made and great fun to drive.

A 1936 PACKARD
Convertible, complete
with rumble seat and a
grand sense of style.

Eastern United States—maintain their exclusivity and high quality by limiting the number of cars on display, usually to around 100. By comparison, Hershey will typically have just under 2,000 cars in the car show! No wonder the first word on everyone's lips is "immense."

Their next word is "variety." The AACA classifies vehicles into 35 classes but then divides those classes until there are 82 separate groups to be judged. Small classes might only have two cars entered, even at an immense show like Hershey; others might have over 100 cars to be judged. It's easy to see how the old car hobby has changed over the years, just by looking at the participation in the classes.

For example, very early electric cars, Stanley steamers and even gasoline-powered cars from the turn-of-the-century do not appeal very strongly to today's enthusiasts. Two or three cars is a large turn-out for such a class at Hershey. On the other hand, classes for Chevrolet Corvettes, '55-'57 Chevies, Ford Mustangs and other "Baby Boomer" cars are chock-a-block with scores, nay hundreds, of cars.

The fastest growing classes are those for muscle cars from the late-sixties, for pickup trucks of all ages, for commercial vehicles and for racing cars of all types. These are the growth classes, the kinds of vehicles that canny investors are buying and savvy collectors are exhibiting. It makes sense. Men between ages 35 and 55, the postwar Baby Boomers, are the ones who are buying and restoring cars today, and they're interested in vehicles they remember as teenagers. Which means '55-'57 Chevies, Mustangs and performance cars of all types.

THE L-HEAD MERCER raceabout was one of the best designs in a group of American sports cars built in the teens and twenties. By 1930, such sports cars were a thing of the past. These Mercers are only a pale shadow of the Finlay Porter-designed T-head Mercers built before World War I, but they are still interesting because of their sporty nature.

CORVETTES ARE NOW considered among the most desirable collector cars of the fifties and constitute a whole class at Hershey. Most beautiful of all are these 1956 and '57 models.

At the same time, the truck market is booming in this country—half of all new passenger vehicles sold each year are trucks, not cars—so naturally this interest in new trucks extends to old trucks, too. Auto racing has grown exponentially to become the largest spectator sport in North America. NASCAR is just one segment of auto racing, and over 5 million people attend a Winston Cup race each year while one out of every three American households watches the races on television. So it's understandable that interest in old racing cars—particularly Indy cars and stock cars—should naturally grow.

Seen from a different perspective, this changing market has created bargains in Brass Era cars, in major classics, in Model T and Model A Fords, in many older "special interest" American cars. If you're intrigued by these machines, now is the time to be buying, not selling.

You don't have to be rich to participate in the Hershey car show. A $24 annual membership in the AACA earns you the right to exhibit in the car show at any AACA National meet; a $15 entry fee gets your car on the Hershey field and a commemorative plaque for your dash. You can exhibit anything from a $3,000 Whizzer motorbike to a $12-million Bugatti Royale.

Preparation for a major car show is as varied as the cars and participants. Wealthy collectors employ permanent curators for their collections, mechanics whose enviable job is to "exercise" the boss's cars and wipe them down afterward. If they're serious—and at this level, life is very serious—such professional mechanics will spend weeks—perhaps months—preparing a car for a particular concours event.

What do they do? On the simplest level, repair any defect that might detract from the car during judging, then clean the car as thoroughly as possible. The finesse comes in the details, and there are even such people as professional detailers who make a career out of cleaning cars for concours. The best detailers start cleaning where you and I would leave off. They use toothbrushes, pipe cleaners and lint-free brushes to clean not just the bodywork and upholstery but the hidden recesses of the engine compartment and even the underside of the chassis.

THE 1934 PACKARD V-12 is one of the great cars of all time. Note the way the shape of the headlight lenses echo the swept-back grille. Superb!

Companies like Armorall, Meguiar's and Mother's Wax cater to concours enthusiasts, and there are special cleaners and polishes for not just paint and chrome, but for leather, vinyl, fabric, rubber and especially brass. Polishing the brightwork on a Brass Era car is a career in itself. Each detailer has his own preferred polish, his own preferred type of cloth. Some recommend waxing the polished brass to protect it from oxidation, some consider that counterproductive, some think it sacrilege.

THE FOUR-CYLINDER, 80 hp T-head engine of this 1904 Peerless racing car has full-pressure lubrication, exposed valve gear and exhaust stubs as big around as your arm.

THE MERCER L-HEAD Raceabout inherited at least some of the panache of its famous T-head predecessor. The Boyce MotoMeter monitors radiator coolant temperature.

THIS SPECTACULAR 1933 Buick 68C Convertible Phaeton is one of the fanciest Buicks ever. It's special because of its unusual four-door convertible bodywork, chrome wire wheels and excellent detailing on a rather mundane chassis that usually carried a dull sedan body.

None of this is difficult. It requires some understanding of materials and their chemical reaction to various coatings, but mostly it requires clean shop towels and elbow grease. For this reason, once the initial expense of a restoration is accomplished, an enthusiastic amateur with lots of free time can score just as well with the judges as a knowledgeable professional.

Getting a prepared car to the car show is an undertaking in itself. No one would consider actually driving a concours quality antique for fear it might be damaged or at the very least, dirtied. Most winning machines arrive like Chinese wives with bound feet, carried in state in their own closed trailers or transporters. There are truckers who specialize in moving these cars, though for a few thousand dollars any car owner can buy an enclosed trailer.

AACA car shows require that the car enter the show field under its own power. But you'd be surprised at the number of important awards that are lost each year because the owner cannot start his engine, usually because gasoline has never been allowed to sully the inside of the gas tank. In a hobby where cleanliness is next to godliness, actually starting your engine might get grease or oil or dirt or coolant on some surface you've just cleaned. So these trailer queens are rarely driven under their own power.

Many car show participants follow a rigid routine. They will have a car

RIGHT UP THERE WITH Corvettes of the same era, two-seater Thunderbirds from '55-'57 are now very collectible. Especially when they're pink or yellow!

SVELTE GRILLE OF THE
1919 Shaw Special track
racer is a sculpture of rare
proportion.

restored, detail it, and then show it in a number of concours over a period of two or three years. By then, the car has won everything it's ever going to win, and it's getting harder and harder to keep it at a concours level. So owners will turn that champion out to pasture. Since they always have at least one other car under restoration, they can start showing that second car. The first one becomes a "driver" for vintage car tours.

Why do AACA members expend so much effort to win a plaque for their bumper? Car shows

are a competitive contest like motor racing or Little League or ballroom dancing. It's satisfying to do it better than anybody else, to be a respected member of an insider's group that most people don't even know exists. There's a strong social side to it, too. The serious competitors know each other, and their shared interest brings them together just like any friendly competitors. They buy and sell each other cars and parts, they share knowledge and mechanics, and most of all, they have a good time doing something they enjoy.

The AACA Eastern National Fall Meet draws everyone from kids who've never seen anything older than Mom's Accord to old car experts who've been around these cars since they were new, back before the Great War. Their levels of understanding are very different of course, but their enthusiasm is equally avid. If there's anything that unites children of all ages, its an old car show. And Hershey is the best in the world.

(ABOVE) 1920 DODGE shows period American flag holder.
(Below) Finlay Robertson Porter's masterpiece, the 50 hp, 1914 T-head Mercer Raceabout, was the sports car to have before World War I. The factory promised it could cover one mile in 51 seconds. Racing versions had a top speed of over 100 MPH.

GET OUT AND GET
under applies to judging
as much as it does to
preparation.

CAR SHOW JUDGING

What is a judge looking for? Well, in most classic car concours, they're evaluating the authenticity of the restoration, the quality of the workmanship, mechanical condition, the overall presentation of the car, and then such subtleties as appropriateness of colors and interiors or the artistic merit of the car itself. At a show like Pebble Beach, for example, Best in Show is rarely going to go to a sedan, no matter how good the restoration, when there are fabulous convertibles and roadsters from which to choose.

The AACA is different. Cars at Hershey compete not against each other but against an ideal standard of excellence that can be applied to any vehicle. The judges are not asked "Is this '55 Thunderbird better than that '55 Thunderbird?" but rather, "How do each of these Thunderbirds measure up against a theoretically ideal Thunderbird?" That is something very different.

Cars in each AACA class are judged on a scale of 400 points. When a car is first shown at an AACA National Meet, it competes in the Junior category. A score of 295 points earns a third, 330 points a second and 365 points a first. If, for example, none of the Junior cars in the class is deemed worthy of 365 points, there will be no first prize awarded. The cars compete not against each other but against the AACA standard of excellence.

After winning a Junior First, competitors move up to the Senior category. A score of 375 points earns a Senior tab for the National First Prize plaque. Senior winners then advance to the Preservation category where 350 points earns a Preservation Award. The whole idea of a Preservation Award is to encourage owners to maintain their cars at a high level rather than allowing them to deteriorate after scoring their Senior First.

This is very important, because show cars are like thoroughbred horses that are brought to their peak of condition the day of a race, then allowed to slack off a little until the next event. A 350 point car can easily be reduced to a 300 point car by incautious driving or neglect. Professional restorers literally prepare for major concours like trainers bringing a winner up to snuff, and a restoration that runs behind schedule so that the car is not ready for the intended show can be a disaster, because unless there is another concours coming along within the next few months, the bloom will go off the restoration, and it will have to be re-prepped. This can be a very expensive business. The Preservation Award encourages owners not to let their cars go but to keep them at a decently high condition and bring them out for other people to enjoy.

HERSHEY JUDGES ARE surprisingly informal. At Pebble Beach and other major concours, judges usually wear white pants, a blue blazer, a white shirt and a tie, like yachtsmen left over from the thirties.

AACA Official Vehicle Classification

1a—3-wheeled vehicles, buckboards, cyclecars not already included in 1b

1b—gas and electric powered mini-vehicles

2—high-wheel, buggy-type vehicles through 1919

3—electric vehicles through 1905

4—electric vehicles from 1906 on

5a—one-cylinder motorcycles

5b—two-cylinder motorcycles

5c—more than two-cylinder motorcycles

5d—motorized bicycles and mopeds

5e—motor scooters

6—steam vehicles through 1905

7—steam vehicles 1906-1914

8—steam vehicles 1915-1929

9a—one-cylinder gas vehicles through 1912

9b—two and three-cylinder gas vehicles through 1912

10a—Ford Model T 1909-1912

10b—Ford Model T 1913-1916

11—Ford Model T 1917-1927

12—gas vehicles not previously classified through 1905

13a—four-cylinder gas vehicles 1906-1909

13b—four-cylinder gas vehicles 1910-1912

14—more than four-cylinder gas vehicles 1906-1912

15—four-cylinder gas vehicles 1913-1919

16—more than four-cylinder gas vehicles 1913-1919

17a—gas vehicles, four-cylinder, two-wheel brakes 1920-1929

17b—gas vehicles, five-seven cylinders, two-wheel brakes 1920-1929

17c—gas vehicles, eight cylinders or more, two-wheel brakes 1920-1929

18a—gas vehicles, four-cylinder, four-wheel brakes 1920-1929

18b—gas vehicles, five-seven cylinders, four-wheel brakes 1920-1929

18c—gas vehicles, eight cylinders or more, four-wheel brakes, 1920-1929

18d—specific Classic vehicles 1925-1927

18e—specific Classic vehicles 1928-1929

19a—specific Classic vehicles 1930-1931

19b—specific Classic vehicles 1932-1933

19c—specific Classic vehicles 1934-1936

19d—specific Classic vehicles 1937-1939

19e—specific Classic vehicles 1940-1942

20a—production vehicles, non-Ford 1930-1931

20b—production vehicles, non-Ford 1932-1933

20c—production vehicles, non-Ford 1934-1935

20d—production vehicles, non-Ford 1936-1937

20e—production vehicles, non-Ford 1938-1939

20f—production vehicles, non-Ford 1940-1945

21a—Ford Model A, open vehicles 1928-1929

21b—Ford Model A, closed vehicles 1928-1929

21c—Ford Model A, open vehicles 1930-1931

21d—Ford Model A, closed vehicles 1930-1931

22a—commercial vehicles, ambulances, funeral vehicles, less than 1 ton through 1927

22b—commercial vehicles, ambulances, funeral vehicles, less than 1 ton 1928-1942

22c—commercial vehicles, ambulances, funeral vehicles, less than 1 ton from 1943 on

22d—commercial vehicles, ambulances, funeral vehicles, 1 ton or more through 1927

22e—commercial vehicles, ambulances, funeral vehicles, 1 ton or more 1928-1942

22f—commercial vehicles, ambulances, funeral vehicles, 1 ton or more from 1943 on

23—fire vehicles

24a—oval, circular or straight course racing cars

24b—road, hillclimb or gymkhana course racing cars

24c—racing motorcycles

25—sports vehicles

26a—production vehicles, non Ford 1946-1947

26b—production vehicles, except 1948 Ford 1948-1949

26c—production vehicles 1950-1951

26d—production vehicles 1952-1953

27a—production vehicles, except Chevrolet 1954-1955

27b—production vehicles, except Chevrolet 1956-1957

27c—production vehicles, except 1958 Chevrolet 1958-1959

27d—production vehicles 1960-1961

27e—production vehicles 1962-1963

27f—production vehicles 1964-1965

27g—production vehicles 1966-1967

27h—production vehicles 1968-1969

27i—production vehicles 1970 on

28a—Ford four-cylinder and V-8 1932-1934

28b—Ford V-8 1935-1937

28c—Ford V-8 1938-1940

28d—Ford six-cylinder and V-8 1941-1948

29—Specific prestige vehicles 1946 on

30—Chevrolet Corvette

31—Ford Thunderbird 1955-1957

32—Chevrolet, except Corvette 1955-1956

33—Chevrolet, except Corvette 1957-1958

34—Ford Mustang

35—limited production and prototype 1946 on

How is a car prepared for judging and how does it "go off?" Well, a major classic restored to Pebble Beach standards—generally considered the highest in the world—will cost anywhere from $200,000 to $1-million, exclusive of the car itself. Literally every part is unbolted from every other part, restored to better than new, then reassembled with so much care that skilled craftsmen will expend at least 2,000 hours on the reassembly alone.

Now imagine if this car—as perfect as time, money and skill can make it— is allowed to get dirty, is transported on an open trailer, or even driven. Now there will be grains of dust in all the crevices, perhaps a slight scuff mark on the seat from the driver's trousers, a minute film of oil from a seeping gasket, or— horror of horrors—a stone chip in the paint or a scratch where the hood rattled against a bracket. Such seemingly insignificant signs of use are enough to drop a 400 point car to 350 points. It will take a professional restorer 20 to 40 hours just to reclean a car that's been rained on or driven across the concours field, working with Q-tips, cotton balls and camel's hair brushes to wipe everything clean. That's how an expensive restoration can "go off" in a matter of moments.

The highest form of AACA judging is in Grand National meets where 360 points earns a third, 370 points a second and 380 points a first in the Grand National Participant category. All Grand National participants scoring over 350 points receive a Preservation Award. Grand National first prize winners advance to the Grand National Senior category. Scoring 390 of a possible 400 points earns a Grand National Senior Award. This can be won repeatedly as long as the owner desires to show the car. On the other hand, keeping any car— no matter how carefully restored—at the 390 point level is both difficult and expensive, even if you are capable of doing it yourself. At the Hershey level it is a formidable task indeed.

Each AACA show judges slightly differently. Hershey has a reputation as being tough, but fair. Judges are members of the AACA who volunteer, on their own money, to travel around the country judging car shows. Obviously, there's a certain gratification to being an AACA judge, and a measurable level of respect from other enthusiasts.

Hershey judging is handled similarly to judging at other AACA National meets. The judges are sent quarterly mailings by the AACA, which include a sign up sheet for different meets. You put down your first choice, second choice, third choice of class that you'd like to judge. The Hershey Region selects the judges it would like from the entries it receives.

Every qualified judge who makes an application to the Hershey Fall meet receives a judging assignment. Of course, you pay your own way to Hershey. When you get to the Hershey show field early Saturday morning, you go to the judge's breakfast and pick up your assignment sheet. You've already been assigned to a judging team, hopefully in the class that you want. Each team has four judges, including a captain and a deputy who is the cosigner of the sheets.

AN ABSOLUTELY SUPERB
1931 Cadillac Convertible
Coupe poses for the
photographers in
Hershey's Winners' Circle.

At Hershey, each team of judges only has to consider 11 cars or less, which are listed on a sheet given to each team captain. Judging is over by late morning, at which point the judges usually wander off to see the other 2,000 cars.

If you keep quiet and out of the way, most judging teams won't mind if you follow them along for awhile, listening to their comments about the various cars. It's like touring the Museum of Modern Art with an art history professor. You'll learn to see the cars in a different way and judge them in a different light.

Judges, of course, are all human and all very individual. The three-tone paint scheme that one judge might find "interesting" another might find "garish" and another consider "unauthentic." But for the most part, since AACA judges have all attended the same judging seminars, the car that one will esteem, all will esteem. The lesson to learn, whether you're an exhibitor, a restorer or just an interested bystander, is exactly how that esteem is earned.

As a general rule, cars which are tasteful but perhaps just a bit flashier than normal will score well. Under AACA rules, a black sedan should score 350

PACKARD APPEAL

I was a partner in a large engineering firm. A few years ago, I went off on my own to work with old cars. So I'm redoing a few cars for other people, redoing one of my own to sell.

This Packard was stored in a barn at Sturbridge Museum, and the barn collapsed. The man who owned the car wasn't in a position to take the car away, so he got Bob Valpey to buy it from him. Bob eventually sold it to me. We didn't dicker over price; the question was whether I was worthy enough.

When I got it, there was a raft of detail work to do.  That can be harder than finding a fender or some other big piece. I have big tables in my garage that were covered with small pieces, pieces that had to be redone and installed before the car was complete. That's what takes the time, not the big things like paint or upholstery. I estimate I've got at least 2,000 hours in this car.

I started with a bare chassis and rebuilt that myself. I redid things like springs, spring hangers, hubs and the multiple disc clutch. The spider gears had to be re-machined. Hundreds and hundreds of teeth had to be filed so that the clutch would not grab when it was engaged.

I made a few concessions. The Burbank cloth that the top was made from is no longer available. So the top cloth is a modern material that looks like the original.

I bought my first Packard for $65 when I was in college. I paid $50 for my second one. I was still in college, and the owner accepted that amount even though it should have been more. I always liked Packards, I guess because they are big, powerful cars with a lot of prestige.
—*Avery Hall*
Car Show Exhibitor

points as easily as a red roadster, but in actual fact, the sportier car will probably earn its Senior First more easily. That's not criticism, just human nature. This makes an AACA meet somewhat self-selecting, in the sense that most people won't bother spend the enormous amounts it takes to produce a Senior First on a car that's not very interesting.

This tends to give us a warped view of the past, to make the past as presented at Hershey grander than it really was. At most car companies, even prestige nameplates like Rolls-Royce, Packard or Cadillac, most of the cars built were practical sedans. Only a small fraction were flamboyant roadsters or convertibles, though to view the cars on display at the typical concours, you'd think most of these companies never built a dull car at all. The old car market reflects all these prejudices: convertibles of most models sell for three or four times the price of the equivalent sedan.

Is this bad, does it matter? Probably not. The cars we're preserving, the best cars in the Hershey concours, are unabashed works of art. Cars that win a Senior First or higher are very close to perfection. Such perfection does not come cheap. Showing cars in old car concours is not a game for the impecunious nor the faint of heart. For which we can only thank the people who are willing to restore and show these cars for the rest of us to enjoy. It's a win-win situation. The owners receive our acclaim, the restorers earn their livelihood, we get to admire their cars.

THE BEST YEAR FOR cars? Many people vote for 1957, when prize-winners like this Chevrolet Bel Air Convertible were built and a continental spare tire kit was a desirable accessory.

NOT EVERYONE'S IDEA of an antique car, this 1962 Volkswagen "bucket truck" attracts more attention than many major classics.

COMMERCIAL VEHICLES

Old cars can be beautiful and elegant and luxurious and works of art. Old trucks are weird and funky and strange and tough and in their own way, works of art. A lot of people are choosing funky over beautiful these days. Why? As many reasons as there are truck enthusiasts, but among them is surely the fact that trucks simply look interesting. They have a whole different aesthetic from automobiles, because they're meant to be, first and foremost, functional.

Trucks are also built for the long haul. Many sports and racing cars are hard to live with, because they were built very lightly when they were new. Parts are fragile, parts are expensive, parts are impossible to find. Not so with trucks. Even the lowliest pickup truck is built with a ten-year life cycle in mind, while heavier trucks and buses are literally meant to last a million miles or a lifetime, whichever comes first.

Among other things, this heavy-duty construction makes restoring and driving an old truck comparatively easy, in the sense that the individual parts are robust and durable and that parts—at least for popular makes—are still available because many of these old trucks are still being used commercially. All of which makes vintage truck ownership easier and cheaper than it might be for a similar automobile.

There are dozens of light-duty trucks from every era well worth restoring for their beauty and charm alone. A '32 Ford pickup, a '40 Ford Sedan Delivery, a '53 Ford F-100, a '51 Chevy pickup, a '55 Chevy pickup or Panel Delivery—all are cleanly styled, timeless designs that will always look good and that will always be popular both with collectors and the guy on the street who comes

AN EXTRAORDINARY 1940 Mack Jr. pickup has everything a commercial vehicle collector could want: it's extremely rare and unusual, good looking, a useful size, beautifully restored and possessed of terrific charm.

A 1925 FORD TT 1-TON has authentic balloon tires on the back and restored Manley hoist. This ought to bring back some fond memories to old garage owners; the TT truck was the universal workhorse of the twenties.

EVERYBODY'S SINGLE favorite vehicle at Hershey is this wonderful segmented tank truck pulled by a 1938 Dodge tractor.

over to say, "Hey, Mister. Nice Truck!". Even better, prices range from under $1,000 to not much over $20,000 for any of the trucks on that list. Not one will ever be worth less than it is right now.

Ford Model TT trucks are a whole topic in themselves. Nothing is as charming as a Ford Model TT; it has all the spindly gawkiness of a young colt, with looks that seem to suggest that some day it hopes to grow up to be a *real* truck. What's most interesting about TTs is that they were the universal workhorse of the teens and twenties, so they were fitted out with an almost bewildering variety of bodies. TTs were everything from motorhomes to furniture movers, from farm trucks to hearses, from tow trucks to fire engines, from dump trucks to buses. At Hershey you'll see the TT in great variety. Values range from under $3,000 to maybe $25,000 for something really special.

At Hershey you'll also see not just pickups and 1-ton TTs but also heavy trucks. The AACA has a class for everything, including tractor-trailers and

Greyhound buses. People actually hunt down these gigantic machines and restore them, just for the satisfaction of having guys like me walk by and say, "Wow. I've never seen anything like that. What is it?" "That's a 1952 Brockway with a Cummins diesel, air brakes and a 13-speed." "Wow!" It goes without saying that something like this is not cheap nor easy to restore, not like a Model TT or a '53 Chevy pickup. But when you're done, you've got a real piece of Americana.

Probably the most popular heavy trucks with collectors are Macks. The famous "bulldog" Macks, the Models AB and AC, are the definitive heavy trucks of the the teens and twenties. They are not sophisticated—Macks still used chain drive as late as 1927—but they have the same snub-nosed appeal as their namesakes. Many of these unbreakable trucks were still in service three or four decades after they were built and earned Mack its bulldog reputation.

Mack also built delectable Mack, Jr. models in the late-thirties, many of which

FORD'S TRUCK MAY have been the most versatile vehicle ever built. This 1921 version was fitted out as a fire pumper for Commack, New York, on Long Island.

THIS BIG OLD OPEN- cockpit American LaFrance pumper was sold in the car corral. Prices for fire equipment are miniscule compared to cars of comparable age and condition.

were given simple pickup bodywork. These little Macks are now very rare—not that many were built—and very collectible. They're larger than Ford and Chevrolet pickups of the time—more like a modern full-size pickup—but with a striking appearance obviously penned by truck engineers, not effete automobile stylists.

American LaFrance is another very collectible nameplate, and like the Ford TT and later Macks, was often used as a chassis for fire equipment. Fire truck collectors form their own sub-group among antique vehicle hobbyists, often more interested in the glitter and off-beat equipment than the vehicle as a vehicle per se. At Hershey, of course, the "truck" half of "fire truck" takes precedence. And what trucks they are.

American LaFrance trucks were always mammoth, powerful and extremely well made. The early six-cylinder models and later V-12s are both superb. And unlike mass-production automobiles, fire trucks are custom-built to last. By the very nature of the business, they must be dependable and rugged, capable of sitting for weeks at a time then roaring off without a warm-up. The typical fire truck has far more stainless steel, aluminum, chrome and brass than more mundane commercial vehicles. There were built as well as anything could be built, at the forefront of the available technology.

THIS FORD FIRE TRUCK is one of the most beautiful commercial vehicles in the AACA. Every detail is perfect.

COMMACK N.Y.

VARIATIONS ON A theme, '50 and '51 Ford F-1 pickups are essentially the same except for the bolder grille on the later model (on right). Both are still powered by the time-honored Flathead V-8, now rated at 100 HP from 239.4 cubic inches.

And fire trucks are cheap. A hulking V-12 American LaFrance from the late-forties or early-fifties is a $3,000 piece of equipment. It probably has less than 50,000 miles on the odometer—fire trucks spend most of their time sitting in a warm garage—and has been meticulously maintained by an enthusiastic group of volunteer firemen. Compared to the equivalent antique car, this is a terrific bargain for what you get.

Should you buy a fire truck? Well, how big is your barn? I know of a

THE NAMESAKE

The only reason that attracted me to this 1936 truck is that it was built by Stewart. Maybe we're related somewhere way back, though I'm from Tennessee and the truck was built in Buffalo. The Stewart company made trucks for 30 years before they went out of business in 1942.

I found my truck right here at Hershey about 20 years ago. The seller drove it here from Baltimore, though it needed a complete restoration. I owned an excavation company, so we restored it in our own shop. Luckily I didn't have to buy many parts, but it still was 12 years in the restoration.

Like a modern truck, this is a component truck. The manufacturer bought all the parts from sub-contractors and assembled the truck. He didn't make many parts himself. This makes it easier to restore. For example, this truck has a Waukesha engine, Clark transmission and differential, Ross steering.

I'm selling it because I went through a divorce last year. I had my drive-out basement decorated like a Ford dealership with eight cars. I'm selling the house, and some cars, too.

—*Jim Stewart*
Car Corral Vendor

really nice American LaFrance aerial ladder truck, complete with ladders, for $2,400. It's cheap because it's 75 feet long and takes two people to steer around corners! The equivalent pumper costs more, because it's small enough to fit in a commercial garage. Should you buy a fire truck? Nothing is more fun. But realistically, a little Ford or Chevy fire truck—or even better a fire chief's speedster built on a truck chassis—will be a lot easier to own.

It's no secret that the two best-selling vehicles in America, year after year, are Ford and Chevrolet pickup trucks. And with good reason. A pickup is the single most versatile vehicle one can buy. The pickup has been popular as long as there have been motorized vehicles. Early light trucks weren't much more than a cart with a motor, but by 1910, Ford was selling a Commercial Roadster—a two-seater with a box in the back that could be used to "pick up" stuff—that was identical in layout and purpose to today's pickup trucks.

It was 1930 before Chevrolet finally introduced a similar Roadster Pickup that was not a car but not a heavy-duty truck, either. By the early-thirties, both Ford and Chevrolet—and many other lesser rivals—had settled on the half-ton load as the proper size for a light-duty pickup, though even back then owners routinely overloaded their trucks just as they do today. That can be a problem for a restorer, of course. The average truck gets worked a lot harder than the average car before it's parked in the barn to rust, so it's usually in much worse shape. Farm trucks are the worst of all. Often they're literally unrestorable because they've received such hard use and poor maintenance.

The first pickups that really drive like modern trucks are the 1953 Ford and 1955 Chevy, thanks to V-8 engines and more advanced suspensions. Not everyone who buys an old pickup wants to show it in a 400 point AACA concours. Most people would rather have a decent-looking truck they can drive and enjoy. For many years I used a restored '57 Chevy as my everyday driver and found it would do everything a new pickup would do except depreciate.

THE 1959 CHEVY 3100 Apache was the deluxe version of the stepside pickup. You can tell by the chrome trim, two-toning and fancier interior.

You can do the same. The first thing to do is decide what you're going to do with your truck once you've got it. If you're planning to show it at AACA meet like Hershey, you probably want something rare and unusual to impress the crowds and the judges. Something like a Mack, Jr. for example. If you're after something that you know will be a sure hit, how about a '40 Ford, one of the prettiest trucks ever built.

If you want something you can actually use and drive, without question your best choice is a post-1955 Chevrolet. These Chevy pickups are all considered collectible, right up into the eighties, particularly such rare models as the big-block Cheyenne of the early seventies or the 454 stepside produced in 1978-1979. Suburbans and pickups from the late fifties—particularly when fitted with four-wheel drive, a rare item back then—are very collectible, too. The queen of Chevy trucks is probably the 1957 Cameo, a limited production luxury model that came with many car-like features, right down to its whitewall tires.

Two interesting subsets under commercial vehicles are the car-based sedan delivery and car-based pickups. Early Ford trucks were car-based, but by the late-twenties, Ford was selling both a truck-based Panel Delivery and a car-based Sedan Delivery. The classics of the sedan delivery genre are probably the '36-'41 Ford and '55 through '58 Chevrolet. Think of them as station wagons without windows, leaving more surface for advertising signage. Sedan deliveries are not only collectible in their own right, but make spectacular tow cars for vintage racers.

In 1957, Ford introduced the Ranchero, the first passenger car-based pickup in decades. Chevrolet responded in 1959 with the El Camino, a similar pickup truck that was essentially a two-door station wagon with the rear of the top cut off. The pretty and useful El Camino stayed in Chevrolet's line-up for years. All of these vehicles—even Ford's Falcon-based Ranchero of the Sixties—are being collected with the usual escalation in prices.

In 1929, Ford introduced the first station wagon, a Model A with simple wooden bodywork that accommodated seats for seven or loads of covered

A PAIR OF INTERESTING Chevrolet trucks from the early-fifties, a 3100 Panel and a Cab-Over-Engine tractor rated at 8 tons GVW. Add the appropriate trailer to either one and you'd have a neat antique transporter.

luggage room. Side-curtains were used in place of windows. The idea was that this rugged wagon could be driven down the the train station and used to pick up both guests and luggage. The woody wagon evolved over the years until by the mid-fifties the only wood left was a wood-grained plastic decal. Any real woody is extraordinarily collectible, with prices that usually far outstrip metal-bodied sedans and convertibles.

The most collectible non-woody station wagon is Chevrolet's '55-'57 Nomad, a svelte styling exercise that for many years was considered the most collectible—and consequently the most expensive—model in the Chevy line from these years. Only recently has the price of convertibles zipped by the price of "Tri-Chevy" Nomads. Ironically, that's the reverse of the trend. Vintage truck and commercial vehicle prices in general are skyrocketing, while prices for many collector cars are stable or falling.

Predictions are that trucks will continue to make up at least 50 percent of the new vehicle market until at least 2010. This should mean that the market for vintage trucks will remain healthy, too. Once people are exposed to new trucks, they naturally get interested in earlier examples, so the demand—and prices— for vintage trucks starts to rise. This is happening right now, and it will continue. Expect to see more and more entries in Class 22 at AACA Concours, more truck-related activity in the swap meet, more trucks in the car corral. Once again, this is a sign of a healthy, growing hobby.

YET ANOTHER VARIANT of the Ford Model T truck, a 1924 Huckster Wagon, originally intended for itinerant retail sales. You can just imagine the rear filled with foodstuffs, housewares or whatever housewives needed.

COMPETITION CARS

For many of us, old racing cars raise the car collecting experience to its highest possible level. For those who prize craftsmanship, most competition machines are hand-built works of art. For those who value technology, racing has always led the way. Just one small example: double overhead camshafts and four valves per cylinder are buzzwords on current production cars. The 1912 Peugeot Grand Prix racer had these features plus desmodromic valve gear and a dry sump, features that still have not made it onto a production passenger car eighty-five years later.

For those who value history, every racing car brings with it an involved story of failure and success. For those who value sports, the heros of motor racing are, in the main, far more interesting and heroic than the stars of stick and ball games. When you make a mistake in tennis, you get hit in the knee with a

FAMOUS INDY 500 driver Fred Frame raced this '33 Ford roadster in the 1933 Elgin Road Races and AAA stock class. This type of "stock car" racing eventually grew into NASCAR and the big-time racing we enjoy today.

MILLER MACHINES: On the left, one of the famous 1935 Miller-Fords built by Harry Miller for Ford Motor Company to race at Indy using a stock-block Ford V-8. In the center, a rear-drive Miller 91 from the late-twenties. This unique machine was fitted with a pair of Miller inline-8s geared together to make a 5-liter U-16 and driven at Indy by Bryan Saulpaugh in 1932. The little Tassi Vatis Kurtis Midget is powered by a 1.5-liter Offenhauser engine originally designed by Harry Miller.

soft rubber ball. Make the equivalent mistake in motor racing, and they cut you out of a chain link fence with power tools.

And so thousands of car collectors have discovered vintage racing cars. The AACA has a class for racers, of course, but the proper place for racing cars is on the track, not parked in a concours. At Friday noon, around 5,000 spectators gather at the Hershey stadium for "race car demonstrations," low speed circuits that give just a hint of what each racer must have sounded like when it was really running at full chat. Still, just to be around these cars, to listen to them idle off the trailer around the track and back on the trailer again at the end of the day, is to grasp in small measure the incredibly powerful hold that racing and racing cars can have on otherwise normal men.

Virtually every type of racing car ever built is being collected by somebody. The grand marques are names like Ferrari, Bugatti, Miller, Kurtis, cars whose pricetags now put them out of reach of most collectors. But you can still buy a Ford-based track roadster from the thirties for less than $20,000, old NASCAR stock cars for less than $15,000, old racing sports cars for less than $10,000, old dirt-track modifieds for less than $3,000. Up until 1970 or so, many racers—especially production-based sports cars—were marginally street legal, which means you can even occasionally drive one to the country club.

A 1935 MILLER-FORD instrument panel—one of the most aesthetically pleasing designs in any racing car.

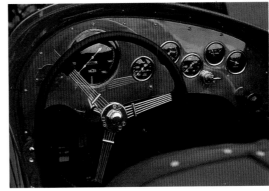

Should you buy a vintage racing car? Emphatically yes. The hot segments are old stock cars, single-seat sprint, Indy, Formula One and "Champ" cars, V-8 60 or Offy Midgets and Trans-Am or Formula 5000 road racing cars powered by raucous Chevy V-8s. The racing cars you see at Hershey are primarily American oval track machines, battered old

GRASSROOTS RACING
in the thirties: a Ford
Model B with OHV
conversion, Stromberg
97s on a Thomas
manifold and one-seater
aluminum body.

THIS 1904 PEERLESS—
sibling of the famous
Peerless Green Dragon
driven by Barney
Oldfield—is a typical
Brass Era race car.

homebuilts from the stock car wars, exquisite single-seaters created by artisans with unlimited budgets.

By far the cheapest type of old racing car you can buy is what's called a modified stock car. You can find them for a few hundred dollars, or even free for the taking. Usually built by amateurs behind the garage, these are typically Ford or Chevrolet coupes from the thirties that have had their fenders cut away, their hoods, glass and interiors removed and the chassis pulled to one side with chains to change the weight distribution. By putting huge tires on the right and small tires on the left, car owners created "stagger" to help them turn left more easily. Engines are typically hot rod Ford flathead V-8s, modified with aftermarket heads, a hot cam and headers. Such cars are cheap, durable and fun.

THIS FORD-BASED DIRT-
tracker features four
individual exhaust pipes
and wonderfully spare
lines so typical of 1933
when this car was made.

By far the most exciting racing cars you'll see at Hershey are the products of the legendary Harry Miller. Miller designs dominated American racing from 1919 until the last Miller-inspired Offenhauser engine ran at Indy in 1980. In the twenties, Miller built both engines and complete cars for Indy and lesser oval track series that were just about unbeatable. In the thirties, Miller built the famous Miller-Ford Indy cars—powered by modified Ford V-8s—and designed the DOHC Inline-4 built by Offenhauser. The famous Offy ruled Indy for five decades.

Most Miller and Offenhauser cars are prohibitively expensive, with prices way over $100,000. The most affordable Miller machine is probably an Offenhauser-powered Midget from the forties or fifties. Offy's little 1.5-liter, DOHC, 150 hp engines were put into tiny single-seaters built by Kurtis, Dreyer, Kuzma and Lesovsky. Such a Midget sells for between $30,000 and $50,000 nowadays.

Early Midgets incorporate all those neat little details that typify many early

MORE GRASSROOTS racing: a tiny Midget racer powered by Ford V-8 60 flathead of 136 cubic inches, sporting three Stromberg 97s. Such racing flatheads typically produce twice the stock engines's 60 HP.

racing cars. Midgets, like most single-seaters up until the seventies, use a single-speed "in-and-out" gearbox like a motorboat, which means, among other things, that they have to be pushed to start. But that extra trouble is just part of their old-time charm. Many of them even still use a hand-operated pump to pressurize the fuel, just like Brass Era passenger cars.

At the opposite end of the spectrum are stock cars. Old stock cars are big, crude and loud, but in their heyday were by far the most popular form of racing in America. At Hershey you'll see things like a 1957 Ford racer, a stripped-out production 1957 Ford two-door sedan with a racing 312 cubic inch V-8. The "factory" stock cars built by Holman and Moody in 1957 used McCulloch super-chargers to produce over 350 HP. Ford dominated NASCAR and USAC in 1957 with cars like these.

Racing cars of any era are special. You'll be amazed at the workmanship, awed by the technology, deafened by the sound and absolutely thrilled by the raw power. Vintage racing is becoming ever more popular, which gives you the option of actually putting your car and yourself on the race track and driving it—at least approximately—at the speeds at which it was meant to be driven. The depth of understanding between you and your car will increase a hundredfold compared to winning yet another concours ribbon.

WHERE TO LOOK FIRST?
1940 Ford Tudor Deluxe
or 1960 Watson sprint car
sponsored by Leader
Cards.

After I get home from Hershey, I need to sleep for a week. It's an exhausting experience.

— **RALPH AVERY**

End of the Day

Hershey is an event. A long, tiring, fatiguing event. Most of us are not used to walking 20 miles a day, living on cheese dogs and chips, constantly looking, thinking and analyzing. Ask most people what they do when Hershey·is over and they'll give you some variation on "Go home and sleep for a week!" Hot baths and soft chairs are also mentioned.

ALL TUCKERED OUT: Charlie expected to get an early start on Sunday morning. When he finally woke up, it was time for lunch.

But before you get to that point, there are the logistics of breaking camp. Hershey starts Monday or Tuesday or Wednesday, depending on who you talk to and how you count. Hershey ends Saturday or Sunday or maybe even Monday, depending on who you talk to and how you count.

The car show is over by 5 P.M. on Saturday afternoon, and for most people, spectators and vendors

DAWN BREAKS OVER A
'55 Chevy, time to close
up shop and head home
until next year.

HEADING HOME FROM the car show, a great variety of cars—and spectators—line the exit of the parking lot. If you really want to experience the car show, this is the way to do it. Instead of walking for miles in the midst of a crowd, just belly up to the barricade, and the car show will come to you.

alike, that signals the official end of the event. You can prolong the moment by standing by the car show exit to watch the machines actually moving under their own power, but all too soon the cars are gone, the AACA officials are gone, the food stands are closed and you're standing alone in an empty parking lot or over by the stadium watching the last stragglers load cars on trailers.

Wander over to the Chocolate Field, and things are almost as melancholy. There are guys pulling down tents, stacking posts, packing boxes, loading trucks, stuffing garbage bags. They're in a hurry, most of them, probably facing a two-day drive to get home for work by Monday morning.

Sunday morning, there are still some die-hard vendors doing business, and the car corral, surprisingly enough, still has hundreds of cars and thousands of hagglers trying to put together that last minute deal. It's significant that the car corral seems to be the first area doing business on Tuesday, the busiest center of activity all week—usually far into the night—and the last place people congregate on Sunday. It's a very healthy sign that the most enthusiasm surrounds the cars themselves, not rusty manifolds or old oil cans.

Over in the swap meet fields on Sunday morning, bargain hunters are swarming over piles of unsold parts that have been simply discarded by their owners, hoping to find that overlooked diamond in the rough. They're still out there Sunday afternoon, picking through garbage in a desultory way. We all find excuses to hang around to watch. Herco's garbage trucks swallow trash. Herco's maintenance men take down snow fencing. The last campers pull down their tents. The last vendors pack up their wares until the next swap meet, the next flea market, the next Hershey.

Coming each October, Hershey marks the end of the old car season for enthusiasts in the Northeast. By the time you get home from Hershey and unload, it's time to start putting your cars away until April, time to start scheduling winter projects for the shop, time to start planning next spring's activities. So there's always a certain sadness in the air, a certain finality that goes along with golden autumn hills and a nip of winter in the early morning air.

Monday morning, except for the occasional antique car still hanging around town while its owners enjoy a well-earned day off, Hershey looks just like it does the remaining fifty-one weeks a year. The transformation from muddy bivouac to pastoral landscape is remarkable for its speed and thoroughness. The invading army comes, it sees, it swaps, it leaves again, causing just the barest ripple on the surface of the normally placid town.

What does the spectacle of Hershey teach us? Many things. Despite what you may have read in mass-market publications still focused on the precipitous fall in Jaguar and Ferrari prices in the early-nineties, despite the threat from environmentalists and general whiners, the old car hobby is not just alive and well, it is prospering like never before. At Hershey alone, there are hundreds of thousands of spectator/buyers from all over the world, thousands of vendors, thousands of exhibitors and total sales that reach into the hundreds of millions.

THE BEST PART OF watching the car show break up is that you'll see each car the way it was meant to be seen, running down the road, not sitting static in a concours row.

It is fashionable among old car enthusiasts lately to wonder aloud, "What will happen to our antique cars when we're gone? Kids today are only interested in computer games!" Our fathers probably worried the same thing about us, and their fathers before them. Then they took us to Hershey.

ONE OF THE GREAT designs from just after WWII, Chrysler's 1949 Town & Country, leaving the Hershey field.

HAULER BEING HAULED: an exquisite 1931 Chevrolet moving van, featuring heavy-duty wheels, heads for home.

Hershey makes you feel encouraged about the future of the hobby. Of course there are more guys with gray hair at Hershey than there are teenagers, but there are also thousands of young people of all ages at Hershey, and they use the same word we used for the same cars a generation ago: "Cool!" We should trust our own instincts. We like old cars. Are our children so different?

A hundred years from now there will still be people buying and selling and trading old cars, just as today they buy and sell and trade paintings that are hundreds of years old. Those future car nuts will probably be a smaller group than we are now, but my money says there will always be people who think a Bugatti, a Ferrari, a Duesenberg is, in its own way, an Old Master as special as a Rembrandt or Vermeer.

Every generation thinks it invented almost everything, from sex to artistic appreciation, from anti-establishment rebellion to loud music. But there are lessons to be learned from people who've come before us, because history does in fact travel in a direction, in cycles, like a ray of light. Our children's children will make the same mistakes we make, delight in the same sensations we delight in. People still watch sunsets, even though for centuries we've known that the sun does not set. Some things, like an appreciation for a beautiful shape or careful hand craftsmanship. like the feeling you get traveling in a convertible— even the pleasure of striking a good bargain on a rare part that you need to finish off your chariot—are the same pleasures people have enjoyed since we first came down from the trees. They're not going to go away overnight.

The main lesson you learn at Hershey is humility. We think we own these cars, we buy and sell and trade them. *Hah.* We are merely caretakers, guardians of history, executors of a public trust. People have been collecting old cars almost since there have been cars to collect. The Bugatti Owners Club was begun in 1928, the AACA itself traces its history to just seven years later. Literally generations of enthusiasts have enjoyed the cars we think of as ours, and it is our responsibility to ensure that more generations will be able to enjoy them after us.

If there is anything one takes home from the Hershey experience, it is that we are all part of this tide of history. When no one remembers what you had to pay for a mint 1953 Texaco oil can or who won class 28D, they'll still be thankful—if they think of us at all—because we went to Hershey, built a hobby, sustained an enthusiasm and saved these old cars. In the end, that is what Hershey is all about, participating in something that is greater than ourselves. Besides, it's fun!

TREASURE HUNTERS sift through stacks of garbage on Sunday morning, looking for overlooked parts that might be restorable or useful. Scenes like this occur all over the swap meet field.

Acknowledgments

A book is like a racing car; one person's name is on the side, but it takes a whole team to make it go.

David Bull of David Bull Publishing came up with the idea for a series on Great American Motoring Events, and chose Hershey as the first event in the series. Tom Morgan of Blue Design created the overall graphic look for the series, while Jean Constantine not only took all the photos but designed this book and did the layouts and mechanicals. She also endured my creative tantrums with understanding and good humor and met impossible deadlines with grace under pressure. If this book had a dedication page, her name would be on it.

David Brownell, Frank Barrett, Bill Smith, Nelson Neff, and James Penhune all read the manuscript for errors, and embarrassingly, found some. Any that are left are my fault, one way or another.

Hundreds of people talked to me about Hershey, too many to list here. Some spoke for just a few minutes, some reminisced for hours. I owe them all a special thank you.

Rich Taylor
Sharon, Connecticut
May, 1997